PREPARING for PEACE

PREPARING for PEACE

– by asking the experts to analyse war

Westmorland General Meeting
Religious Society of Friends, known as Quakers

British Library Cataloguing in Publication Data

A catalogue record for this book is available from the
British Library

ISBN

Cover Design: Paul Airy (www.fourninezerodesign.co.uk)
Printed by Bell and Bain Ltd., Glasgow

The diabolical concept that in order to have peace we must prepare for war has been ingrained in us since the start of civilization.

Professor Sir Joseph Rotblat, 2001,
The Quest for Global Peace

Let him who desires peace prepare for war.
Igitur qui desiderat pacem, praeparet bellum.

Flavius Vegetius Renatus 375 AD, De Rei
Militari

The Preparing for Peace planning group is grateful to
Charlotte Hubback, publishing co-ordinator, Peter Little,
production consultant, and Sheila Jacobs, for their
generous assistance in producing this book

CONTENTS

Preface

Preparing for Peace began in July 2000 at Rookhow in the English Lake District. Rookhow is a Quaker Meeting House surrounded by woodland and hilly sheep pastures. Its origin is symbolic of the aspiration in *Preparing for Peace:* in 1725 the local Quakers worshipped at three different meeting houses all a day's horse-ride apart, which meant they could not meet together on a single day for worship. The solution was unusually rational: a fourth meeting house was built at the point equidistant from the three meeting houses, to provide a common meeting place, only half a day's ride away. Today it is a hostel, as well as a meeting place for Quakers from Westmorland General Meeting which draws Quakers from seventeen local meetings, stretching from Chorley in Lancashire to the south, and Ambleside in Cumbria to the north. It is to our capacity for reason that *Preparing for Peace* speaks.

Professor Sir Joseph Rotblat, the physicist and Nobel Peace Prize winner was the guest speaker in July 2000. His words impacted strongly on those present. He spoke of human beings as an endangered species, put at risk by the nuclear weapons we have invented. He had never been a pacifist but he had concluded nevertheless that this meant war must cease to be an approved social institution, that it had no place in today's world. Our world now had many of the features of a global community and this helped to make it possible for us to say that 'a world without war is an idea whose time has come'.

With this inspiration Westmorland Quakers decided to follow up what Joseph Rotblat's ideas meant for the modern Quaker position on peace. This is most succinctly expressed in the injunction to live 'in the virtue of that life and power that takes away the occasion for all wars'.[1] Could we examine the worldwide assumption that armed conflict is a sensible way in the twenty-first century for settling national and international disputes?

A small group came forward to plan the project, in Quaker terms 'acting under concern'. The ideas striking us forcibly were that the technology of war had become horrific in terms of its potential for annihilation, and that, even without nuclear devastation, the viability of war as a way to solve problems was itself annihilated by its excoriating human, economic and environmental costs. The approach agreed upon was to investigate the proposal that war was redundant as a means of resolving conflict, by inviting experts in their fields, mainly non-Quakers and non-pacifists, to address a set of questions.

The questions are

- Why are people willing to go to war?
- Is war successful in achieving its objectives?
- Can war be controlled and contained?
- What are the human, economic and environmental costs of war?
- How can the world move forward to another way?

It was planned as a three-year programme of public lectures and additional papers, culminating in publication of the findings. Funds would be required. In addition to a grant by the Joseph Rowntree Charitable Foundation, an independent social policy research and development charity, donations have been received from the R.H. Southern Trust (a family trust), over one hundred local Quaker meetings and many individuals.

In the course of the programme, all the papers delivered at lectures or otherwise, have been published on the website

www.preparingforpeace.org

The website is an open-ended project with new papers which underpin or develop these themes, continuing to be published. There is a similarly open-ended teacher's project developing materials based on the papers, which assist teachers of citizenship in schools; in addition, a study aid entitled 'The Anatomy of War' will be published later this year. Twelve lectures and twelve papers form the basis of the present volume. Space has permitted only six lectures and two papers to be included here.

The planning group was repeatedly heartened by the generosity of the project's contributors, all busy people bearing heavy responsibilities, who wrote papers or travelled to the north of England to speak at meetings, and sought no payment for their time. Each lecture, whether it was held in Kendal, Lancaster or Preston, was well attended and evoked a lively questions session.

It is now our aspiration to bring the results of these enquiries to the attention of decision-makers worldwide, believing that, for them, like us, their ideal is a peaceful world, even though they believe the means to be debatable or elusive. Equally we offer our findings to our fellow citizens in the hope they may find them useful in formulating their own positions, and advancing their ideas within their own social groups and political constituencies. We publish eight sample papers in this volume. We hope readers will seek out the others on our website where they are available in printer-friendly versions. *Preparing for Peace* is an invitation to continue a process of rational enquiry about making our world a peaceful place.

The tragic events of 11 September have reminded us that 'No man is an island', no country can isolate itself from all the others. Our quest must be for global peace; because peace is indivisible; there cannot be peace in one part of the globe while war, or acts of terrorism occur in another part. We live in a world of ever-increasing interdependence of all inhabitants of the earth, an interdependence largely due to the advances in science and technology. Globalization – whether in its positive or negative aspects – has brought about a situation whereby events in any part of the globe affect us all: in economic, cultural, or political issues, and certainly in military matters; in matters of war and peace.[2]

Professor Sir Joseph Rotblat,
September 2001

Introduction

The central argument of the *Preparing for Peace* project is simply stated: war does not work as a tool of politics in the twenty-first century. War does not work because it can no longer produce the results that political and military leaders hope to gain from using it; it carries a disproportionate level of risk to social stability and human security; and it is fundamentally incompatible with our transformation into a stable, global community. Our populations are interrelated through economies, communications and the media, migration, tourism, health, employment and a shared natural environment. Inevitably, war and violence in one corner of our world affect the security of systems and communities far distant, as Professor Sir Joseph Rotblat suggests when he describes peace as 'indivisible'. When the theatre of war spans our globe, no one can be assured of immunity. Moreover, the human, environmental and economic costs of modern war cannot be reconciled with our stated aim to uphold civilian immunity, to protect vital ecosystems, to eradicate poverty and famine, or to control the scourge of diseases such as HIV/AIDS.

In the new circumstances in which we find ourselves at the beginning of the twenty-first century, civil society is justified in asking its leaders to reject war as a means of resolving disputes. In doing so, we do not expect to extinguish acts of violence around the world. But there *is* a realistic prospect of removing the credibility and legitimacy of war in the international arena, just as institutions such as slavery, segregation, apartheid and child labour – once thought to be immutable and a 'natural' consequence of social hierarchy – were discredited and outlawed across the nineteenth and twentieth centuries.[3] Slavery and segregation have not yet disappeared, but it is inconceivable that the international community would promote or condone them. We need to ensure that war is moving on the same trajectory.

In making these arguments we acknowledge that we are asking leaders to consider war in a new way. How is it possible for war to be out-of-date? Many of us believe that war is a part of the human condition, an inevitable consequence of human relations, or even genetically determined. The military-industrial-scientific complex is testimony to this belief, symbolic of our constant preparedness for an unspecified but 'inevitable' war. But this belief has little basis in fact. The Seville Statement gives authority to the view that war is not integral to our nature.[4] It is not explained by human aggression as our contributor Professor Robert A. Hinde states so clearly, 'The psychological and physiological mechanisms that cause one individual to strike another have nothing in common with the chains of command in an invading army.'[5] Nor is it an impersonal physical event, like a tidal wave, which humankind is powerless to resist or stop. Wars occur when sufficient people are organised in armed combat. Indeed, even in its most brutal and chaotic aspect, war is an organised and institutional form of violence. Warfare is essentially a problem-solving device that leaders have turned to during key periods in history, usually in the context of perceived threats to survival and identity, to themselves or to the people they lead. Such threats will continue to arise, but the range of problem-solving devices open to us has grown exponentially in the course of the twentieth and early twenty-first centuries. We have transformed the context within which political decision-making occurs, with the development of international humanitarian law, multi-lateral and regional institutions, and sophisticated methods of conflict prevention and resolution. Today there are credible alternatives to war. We have been encouraged to note that many senior military officers and strategists endorse the need to seek solutions free of military intervention,[6] as in the late Brigadier General Michael Harbottle's *Proper Soldiering* and the publications of the organisation Generals for Peace. Political leaders must therefore see themselves within the context of history: they have both the necessity and the prospect of rejecting this tool of politics.

The purpose of this book is to summarise our argument that modern war is ineffectual and increasingly irrational. In doing so we use the term 'war' in its broadest sense. We do not underestimate the complexity of the phenomenon we call 'war'. It encompasses different types of conflict (symmetrical and asymmetrical war, inter- and intra-state war, and terrorism), and requires case-specific approaches and solutions. Our purpose has been to point to the urgency of finding peaceful solutions to political differences, and to draw on those aspects of our authors' texts that we believe are most innovative and relevant. Our authors have different opinions on the use and future of war as a political tool, on whether war can or cannot be abolished, on whether war works.

The book is split into five main parts. The first part looks at our reasons for declaring war an ineffectual and irrational tool of politics. The second part explores ways towards peaceful solutions and informed leadership. In the third, we put forward our conclusions. Part Four provides an outline of each of the papers published on the website, with a cut off date of 31 March 2005. Finally, in the fifth, we present eight sample papers.

PART ONE

IS WAR A RATIONAL TOOL OF POLITICS?

The most important insight might be the simple yet profound idea that war is redundant, obsolete, and demonstrably unsafe as a tool of diplomacy. I would go so far as to say that our principal task at the start of the twenty-first century is to promote that idea.[7]

Brian W. Walker,
Former Director-General of Oxfam

War is widely acknowledged to be a blunt and unpredictable tool. It is increasingly seen as irrelevant to the problem it tries to address in the twenty-first century. Even within war-minded administrations there are often strict conditions determining when it is possible for war to be employed. One condition that is central, is a realistic prospect of success. Indeed, implicit in the use of war as a tool of politics, even as a 'last resort' or as a 'lesser evil', is the notion that the objectives of those prosecuting military action will be achieved; that political and military leaders can contain war within desired limits and borders; and that the benefits of war will outweigh the human, economic and environmental costs. Moreover, in today's global media environment, war has to be *seen* to be succeeding if political reputations are to remain intact. As Professor Hew Strachan suggests, 'Much of the readiness to threaten or use force globally rests on pragmatism rather than ideology.' Yet it is on the question of pragmatism that war most obviously fails as a tool of politics today.

When we talk of success we are not talking of war as a strategic operation only, but as an ethical decision. Importantly, pragmatism lies at the heart of ethical codes. The Christian Just War doctrine is perhaps the most explicit: for example, clause 4 *Probability of success: Arms must not be used in a futile cause or in a case where disproportionate measures are required to achieve success.*[9] For many leaders, decision-makers and military personnel, pragmatism and ethics are inseparable: war must only be used to prevent or rectify a grave public evil and it must only be used if it is likely to achieve that objective. But we might ask, can war – whether strategic or ethical in intent – actually work today? It is evident to us that modern war fails the test of pragmatism and ethics. We have outlined our four principle reasons, below.

1

Modern war cannot achieve the objectives leaders hope to gain from it

It is clear that more and more individuals worldwide are realising that war does not solve conflict, nor resolve long-standing cycles of violence.[10]

Dr Scilla Elworthy
Founder of the
Oxford Research Group

The objectives for which modern war is waged are rarely met. As can be seen in Professor Beatrice Heuser's analysis for *Preparing for Peace*, war in the post-1945 world became increasingly difficult to prosecute effectively, ethically and conclusively. Superpowers and their allies suffered a dismal lack of victories and struggled to reconcile military strategy with an apocalyptic vision of how a nuclear attack might unfold.[11] With the benefit of hindsight, we can see that much of the evidence emerging post-1945 pointed to the political and moral wisdom of avoiding war.

This view is taken up by certain of our authors. According to Brian Walker, 'In modern war the declared aims of the conflict are rarely attained. Vietnam, Suez, the West Bank, India/Pakistan, Afghanistan and Iraq – each testifies to this stern judgement. Twenty-first century war, on the whole, simply doesn't work.'[12] And in the course of his paper on environment and war, Professor John Cairns Jnr describes a new paradigm in which there is no longer such a thing as success:

> The wars of the twenty-first century have not produced the elation that followed the end of World War II. No heads of nation-states surrendered and acknowledged defeat. In fact, victory was not announced as it was at the end of World War II. Instead, words such as 'cessation of hostilities' were used, even though significant portions of the populations of Afghanistan and Iraq have remained hostile and many indigenous combatants have merely discarded their uniforms and hidden their weapons, almost certainly with the intention of using them at the first opportunity. Diplomatic relationships of long standing have been replaced with suspicion and lack of trust.[13]

The impotence of the traditional war doctrine has been heightened by the rise of terrorism in the late twentieth century and early twenty-first century. It is difficult to envisage a military solution or final victory in places such as Chechnya, Afghanistan or Iraq. Nor is it possible to identify the limits to the theatre of war. Should atrocities in Casablanca, Madrid, Bali, Istanbul and Beslan be considered a part of these wars? Paradoxically, 'shock and awe' technologies and military power cannot extinguish asymmetrical warfare and global terrorism, and may indeed act as a stimulus. Professor Hew Strachan's concern for the new global reach of war and violence – the ability to 'strike back' anywhere in the world with almost any form of weaponry[14] – is widely shared among our authors. According to Professor Paul Wilkinson, a chain reaction of military and terrorist responses might result in weapons of mass destruction being used. Terrorism's effectiveness rating is no better, however, in that he observes that the objectives of terrorism are seldom met.[15]

Among our experts General Sir Hugh Beach makes the strongest statement for the success of war when he says it is usually not successful but it can be the lesser of two evils. His case example of the Kosovo War provides evidence which would point some to a different conclusion in that instance. More tellingly he gives the example of General Dallaire, commander of the UN forces in Rwanda in 1994, who requested three battalions to avert the genocide of 800,000 Tutsis, and was refused.[16] For some the notion of war with strictly defined humanitarian objectives remains a convincing idea.

The strategic problem facing contemporary leaders is that military power cannot guarantee national or human security. Neither conventional warfare nor the notion of a 'war on terrorism', are effective against terrorist threats, and cannot be contained within a single theatre of war.

2

Modern technologies of war cannot be controlled or contained

We have become too good at war, and it now amounts to potential suicide.[17]

Dr Chris Williams and Yun-Joo Lee

A second major strategic and ethical crisis facing political and military leaders is their inability to contain the technologies of modern war. This lack of control and containment takes several forms: weapons proliferation around the globe; risks of harm from the testing and deployment of existing nuclear, biological and chemical weapons; and the development of new weapons of mass destruction, promising ever more deadly forces. Modern war contains within it a higher level of risk than has ever been known in the history of war, including the risk of human extinction.

Weapons proliferation is a critical concern for many of our authors, including Professor Robert A. Hinde, Professor Paul Rogers, Professor M.S. Swaminathan and Sir Samuel Brittan.[18] The demise of the Cold War has seen a flood of cheap small arms onto world markets. M.S. Swaminathan argues that, 'The dramatic increase in the availability and use of small arms has become a highly destabilizing factor, both in industrial and developing countries.'[19] But the proliferation of *nuclear* weapons is especially worrying, with over thirty thousand nuclear weapons in existence and a potential black-market in enriched uranium.[20] Critical to arms proliferation is the support and importance given to the military-industrial-scientific complex among developed countries, with a concomitant and dubious perception that the costs to government are offset by arms sales. The arms trade is, in Robert A. Hinde's view, the 'Achilles heel' of the complex, in being the least amenable to regulation.[21] Dr Chris Williams and Yun-Joo Lee remind us that 'Many conflicts have shown how weapons can end up being used against their manufacturers and their allies.'[22]

The risks posed by modern weapons technology are also prohibitive. Despite a stated preference for 'precision-guided' missiles and 'smart' technology among world leaders, the world's arsenal now includes nuclear, biological and chemical weapons whose effects could, if deployed, reach far beyond a single region or nation, and threaten self-annihilation for the aggressive force: a strategic dead-end. The nuclear threat, often consigned to history with the end of the Cold War, is still real, and possibly increasing. Professor Swaminathan suggests: 'There is a real danger that nuclear weapons will once again be used in conflicts currently growing in seriousness.'[23] Our inability to control and contain the technologies of war is also the theme of Professor Sir Joseph Rotblat's paper. His thesis is that in our peculiarly global age, the impact of war is global

> The chief characteristic of the nuclear age is that for the first time in the history of civilization we have acquired the technical means to destroy our own species, and to accomplish it, deliberately or inadvertently, in a single event. In the nuclear age the human species has become an endangered species.[24]

To the risk of technological threats we could add the risk of technological vulnerability, as mentioned by Dr Chris Williams and Yun-Joo Lee in their paper.[25] The bombing (accidental or deliberate) of nuclear power plants, chemical factories, oil installations, or even scientific laboratories, has implications for human health, agriculture and the natural environment over a wide area. Peacetime disasters at Chernobyl and Bhopal, and the wartime firing of oil installations during both Gulf wars, have given us some idea of how such catastrophes might unfold.[26]

But perhaps the greatest concern is the fact that the development of *new* omnicidal technologies continues. M.S. Swaminathan, again: 'Scientific findings are being used to perfect weapons of mass destruction and fear of each other is growing because of the emergence of new methods of mass killing like the release of lethal strains of small pox and anthrax as well as suicide bombing'.[27] 'The root cause of our problem today lies in the growing mismatch between technological progress and ethical and spiritual evolution.'[28] Brian Walker likewise fears scientific developments in the field of war, and what these developments tell us about political policy and morality in the twenty-first century.[29]

It is evident that war has outgrown first the ethical and then the strategic limits through which the international community has previously tried to rationalise and control war. In modern war, protagonists risk a technological holocaust or an endless cycle of asymmetrical violence arising in any part of the world. In a world awash with weaponry – from small arms to lethal strains of bacteria – leaders simply ought not to risk war. We should rather be turning our efforts and resources towards reducing and removing the production, sale and availability of weapons, towards *limiting* arms as we seek alternate and peaceful methods for solving disputes between nation states.

3

War carries new political and legal risks for leaders

Soon after the Pinochet affair, the dictator of Ethiopia had to flee South Africa, where he was receiving medical treatment, because Human Rights Watch in New York publicised that he was there.[30]

Judge Richard Goldstone
Former Chief Prosecutor, UN International Tribunals

The idea that war is a rational tool assumes a political vacuum. But twenty-first century leaders do not exist in a vacuum. They have diminishing autonomy. They operate within the context of domestic political pressures, international law *and* a global media; and their actions and decisions are noted by a spectrum of fellow leaders, governments, non-governmental organisations, multinational companies and multilateral institutions such as the UN. As Dr Chris Williams and Yun-Joo Lee suggest, all wars now have a 'regional' context.[31]

It is becoming increasingly obvious that live news reporting and global information networks, such as the internet, are diminishing the power and usefulness of war as a tool of politics because they are changing the way in which we witness war. At the time Karl von Clausewitz was writing *On War*, a battle or even a war itself was likely to be over before a detailed account of events and casualties reached a wider audience. In contrast, our leaders live in a world where the process of waging war is opened to live scrutiny; a world where people can access independent information from innumerable sources; a world in which political and military leaders are called on to explain a multitude of individual incidents as they happen. Dr Paul Grossrieder points out that 'the images of atrocities in the former Yugoslavia, in Somalia and Rwanda were part of our mental geography in the 1990s.'[32]

Public scrutiny is particularly problematic when it captures those moments of abuse which seem to be inherent in the chaos of war: global media coverage of human rights abuses at Abhu Graib prison in Iraq were deeply damaging to the Coalition's moral case for war. But even a humanitarian objective can fare poorly against the immediacy of live reporting. Our author General Sir Hugh Beach – who sees a humanitarian role for war in line with the Christian Just War doctrine – acknowledges this when he asks, 'How likely is it that, as the price of success mounts, the political constituency, nurtured on television, will lose patience and enforce a humiliating withdrawal, leaving things worse than if force had never been used?'[33]

In addition, the legal consequences of modern war are multiplying. War-minded leaders around the world vary in their attitude towards international law, but they all now live with the *possibility* that they might one day be held to account for their actions, whether for human rights abuses or for war crimes committed at home and abroad. The Yugoslavia and Rwanda tribunals have made this point clear. Even those who evade charges or arrest might nevertheless find their freedom and quality of life in jeopardy. Judge Richard Goldstone notes that in the wake of General Pinochet's arrest in England in 1998 under the Torture Convention, 'Many other oppressive dictators around the world began to have problems travelling.'[34] But it is not just 'dictators' who are at risk. According to Judge Richard Goldstone, leaders in the Western world also have a fear of being branded war criminals, and indeed he attributes growing pressures to limit civilian casualties to the effectiveness of 'War Crimes Tribunals and the publicity given to war crimes'.[35]

Any leader or indeed government contemplating war in the twenty-first century must take seriously the political and legal consequences that might ensue from a war, or from breaches of the Geneva Conventions by their forces. And the spectrum of war crimes continues to expand. As a consequence of the Yugoslavia and Rwanda tribunals, systematic rape has also been recognised as a war crime, and in certain circumstances as a form of genocide.[36] The problem contemporary leaders have is that they cannot predict how legal sensibilities will change in the future, reclassifying actions committed today as war crimes tomorrow. The long-term consequences of their actions are unknown. And as the Pinochet case has shown, leaders accused of breaking international law cannot assume there is a time limit to the threat of prosecution or legal action under domestic *or* international law. It is a risk that leaders are going to be increasingly unwilling to take as international humanitarian law develops in sophistication and reach.

So far we have considered structures of international law. But there is another legal risk for those taking military action. Leaders, governments and armed forces must now expect to face lawsuits from the national or regional governments affected and even from civilians themselves. In just one such case, in December 2004, the British High Court ruled that there must be a full independent inquiry into the September 2003 death in custody of a twenty-six-year-old Iraqi citizen at the hands of British troops in Basra, southern Iraq. His family had sought a judicial review, arguing that the government was in breach of the European Convention on Human Rights and the UK Human Rights Act 1998 by not conducting an independent enquiry into the deaths. Whether they are successful or not, an unremitting course of legal cases and legal questions is debilitating to political and military reputations; if any such cases *are* successful, the political and economic repercussions are likely to be profound. Indeed, it seems that the enormous potential of such suits is only just beginning to be understood. It is likely that all future wars will be followed by claims for the death and injury of individuals, and large-scale claims for structural, environmental and economic damages suffered in war. Again, we believe it is a risk that seriously diminishes the usefulness of war as a tool of politics.

Advances in media technologies and legal powers have brought innumerable benefits. They have encouraged greater protection for civilians and have led to enquiries and prosecutions where abuses have occurred: factors which are widely welcomed by the international community and by many military forces around the world. But they have not helped leaders in their use of war. Indeed, we are entering a context in which the risks of political and legal fallout from war are putting it out of reach altogether.

4

Modern war is incompatible with human security and social stability

Since 1945, 84% of the people killed in wars have been civilians.[37]
Dr Paul Grossrieder,
Former Director General of the International
Committee of the Red Cross

The impact of modern war on human security and social stability takes a number of different forms. The most obvious and immediate is death and injury in war. Obvious it may be, but it is hard to assimilate that 160 million people were slaughtered in war in the twentieth century.[38] Combatants and non-combatants alike are affected, but it is important to remember that in the last half century civilians have been generally ten times more at risk of death in war than combatants.[39] It is important, also, to realise that numbers of casualties are only *one* index by which we can measure the impact of war. When we discuss civilian immunity, stability and security (or, conversely, so-called 'collateral damage') we should also include the wider social, environmental and economic costs of war.

Numbers of civilian deaths and injuries are often the critical measure by which a military operation is deemed just or valid. Many military powers operating today make a greater effort to avoid civilian casualties than was the case in the middle or later decades of the twentieth century. Some of our authors have pointed to a general *intention* to limit deaths during operations in Kosovo and Afghanistan, as compared to Vietnam and Korea, for example.[40] Such efforts are undoubtedly a result of the growing body of international law and increasing media scrutiny, and are to be welcomed as proof that humanitarian law and freedom of information are gradually putting war out of reach. Yet the question of proportionality remains. What is a 'low' civilian death count? How could more deaths be avoided? Is an *intention* to avoid civilian casualties enough? As has been shown in the recent wars in Afghanistan and Iraq, though the intention is to avoid harm to civilians, unreliable intelligence can result in the bombing of civilian centres such as market-places and wedding parties. And despite having put so much emphasis on their intention to minimise civilian suffering in the Iraq war, coalition forces have yet to supply accurate numbers of civilian casualties.[41]

Inevitably, the degree of protection offered to civilians largely depends on the weapons and military strategies used. Continuing attachment to indiscriminate technologies seems to indicate a profound inconsistency in attitudes towards civilian immunity. For example, possession and development of 'weapons of mass destruction' such as nuclear, chemical and biological weapons, even by states that purport to abide by the Geneva Conventions, suggests a fundamental denial of civilian immunity. So too does the continuing use of 'conventional' strategies and weapons with a long-term and indiscriminate impact, such as uranium-tipped shells, cluster-bombs, high-altitude bombing and anti-personnel land-mines.[42] Even 'precision' or 'smart' technologies are dependent on accurate intelligence and a clear separation between civilian and combatant infrastructure on the ground: an impossibly perfect state of war. In short, as pressure to avoid civilian casualties in war mounts, the impossibility of doing so becomes more apparent, the 'surgical' strike more elusive. Brian Walker concludes that 'just war' principles of proportionality and non-combatant immunity 'collapse as unattainable in modern war when civilians are ten times more at risk of death than soldiers.'[43]

Calculating numbers of deaths is not the only means of assessing the human cost of war. It is to Dr Grossrieder's paper which we must turn for a holistic insight into 'the core problem of war', namely, the 'tragic effects on individuals and communities.'[44] As Dr Grossrieder shows all too clearly, the human cost of war has many guises. In addition to death and injury in war, civilian populations also suffer the immediate and long-term consequences of displacement, separation of families, sexual violence, torture, disease, hunger, unemployment, loss of education and healthcare, and loss of those personal objects that signify stability and identity: 'whole societies are deeply shattered', says Grossrieder.[45] Displacement is perhaps the most visual problem. At the time of writing, some 24 million people are displaced within their own countries, and a further 18 million are displaced across their national borders, as a result of conflict.[46] In contrast, other harmful and protracted consequences of war are invisible. Psychosocial trauma ensuing from exposure to war and violence is a form of 'collateral damage' which is largely unaccounted for because it is impossible to measure.[47] Indeed, it is striking that even states which have developed exhaustive laws and systems to protect innocents (particularly children) from physical and psychological harm, simultaneously engage in and uphold war, an activity in which such harm is a daily reality.

To the human and social costs of war, we must add environmental costs. There are extraordinary stories of postwar regeneration in the built and natural environment, but there are also examples of long-term contamination and harm, whether as a result of the weapons used (such as defoliants, radioactive materials and munitions) or as a result of the infrastructure that has been damaged (such as oil installations, chemical factories and dams). For example, Professor Rogers notes that lands laid with land-mines in North Africa during the Second World War are still out of use; Cairns points to the oil which encrusted a quarter of the Kuwaiti desert after the first Gulf War, contaminating essential aquifers.[48] Rogers also reminds us that environmental damage is not simply a matter for the theatre of war: we must also consider the pollution resulting from weapons industries and weapons testing.[49] And we are reminded that warfare *consumes* limited natural resources in the form of fuels and materials. Thus, by both damaging and consuming natural capital, war adds to existing ecological crises and creates new ones. Cairns, a scientist, is unequivocal when he states that 'War is an unsustainable practice on a finite planet with finite resources.'[50]

What of the economics of war? In 2001 global military expenditure exceeded $839 billion or $137 per global citizen.[51] In 2002 the value of all arms transfer agreements worldwide was nearly $29.2 billion.[52] Estimates vary for the projected costs of US military action in Iraq, but on 8th April 2004 the BBC reported an estimated final bill in excess of $300 billion.[53] Another perspective is how the

> UK has allowed the military nexus to dominate its science base. Last year (2004) the UK allocated a third of all science research (£2.6 billions), to exotic, weapons based, high technology. The military research budget absorbs, in fact, 30% of all public research & development budgets. Yet the military spends only 6% of that budget on conflict prevention.[54]

To the cost of engaging in war must be added the cost of cleaning-up damaged environments and restoring shattered communities *after* war. For example, according to Professor John Cairns, the United Nations is involved in processing more than US$ 70 billion in claims for environmental damages during the invasion of Kuwait in the first Gulf War.[55]

Moreover, military spending itself is highly inefficient. As Dr Grossrieder suggests, the costs of prevention compare favourably with the costs of war. He notes that prevention peacekeeping in Macedonia cost US$ 8 million (July 2002), whilst the cost of NATO intervention in Bosnia in 1996 was some US$ 134 million. He claims: 'If States ever seriously compared the costs of war with those of prevention, they would recommend that their foreign ministries negotiate, in the Security Council for example, preventative deployments of peacekeepers.'[56] Dr Scilla Elworthy similarly argues that late intervention in crises can cost between twice and ten times that which early intervention would have cost.[57] Subsidy and support of arms exports by many states is also economically irrational, as economist Sir Samuel Brittan shows in his paper on the UK arms trade.[58]

We come, then, to what might be deemed the true 'collateral' impact of war. To appreciate this we must think of security in a more sophisticated way. Human security rests on safe, sustainable and healthy livelihoods, factors which in turn depend on multilateral efforts towards sustainable development and peaceful processes of change. War is fundamentally incompatible with these conditions and processes. As we have seen above, war compromises or destroys local efforts towards sustainable development through damage to agriculture, trade, education and health. War also hampers international efforts. Development and health NGOs and agencies cannot achieve their long-term objectives in volatile societies: Dr Grossrieder notes that displacements through conflict 'undermine all efforts undertaken to improve people's lives within their own countries.'[59] It is not just development that is affected, but also global communications and trade. Aside from those companies who profit from defence contracts and post-war reconstruction, the *majority* of industries, trades and multinational companies require stability and security in order to conduct their daily business. War is simply not in their interests.

But perhaps the greatest 'collateral' cost is in allocation of resources. War diverts vast political, economic and scientific resources away from the core problem of global survival on the planet towards contrary processes of damage and destruction. Numerous of our authors, including Brian Walker, John Cairns Junior, M.S. Swaminathan and Crispin Tickell argue, as we do, that war in the twenty-first century is counterproductive to more important political objectives.[60] Sir Crispin Tickell says 'Wars must not be allowed to crowd out, even temporarily, the need to think about the big issues and work together in trying to resolve them.'[61] In Cairns' opinion, humankind will have to choose between war and sustainable development.[62]

In conclusion, growing pressure to reduce the human impact and cost of war is serving to show how impossible such an ideal is: the human, economic and environmental costs of modern war are fundamentally incompatible with notions of civilian immunity and human security. Moreover, war erodes human security and social stability at a time when such factors are essential to resolving the global threat of disease, poverty, hunger and environmental crisis. The global community cannot afford war in the twenty-first century.

Summary of Part One

Can war still be considered a feasible, valid or rational tool of politics in the twenty-first century? It seems evident to us that the emerging answer to this question must be 'no'. We live in a new political and technological context in which previous strategic and ethical uses of war have been rendered redundant. It is becoming increasingly difficult for leaders to prosecute war with any certainty of political success or even political survival, as they struggle to keep war within legal, moral and even geographical limits. Most importantly, war is fundamentally incompatible with expectations of stability and security in human, environmental and economic terms.

PART TWO

ALTERNATIVE RESPONSES TO THE THREAT OF WAR

Alternative Responses to the Threat of War

Effective tools and strategies to replace war depend upon a true analysis of what is driving it today. Collectively and with high levels of consistency our authors have identified the features which constitute the major threats to peace in the twenty-first century. These emerge in two categories. We will look first at these threats and then at ways of responding to them. First the direct threats arising from war-like action

- Unilateralism and preventive war
- Terrorism and the war on terrorism
- Civil war and low intensity conflict

Secondly, the threats arising from the factors which create the conditions for war

- Deteriorating environments and the competition for natural resources
- Poverty and injustice
- Availability of weapons across the spectrum from small arms to weapons of mass destruction

Unilateralism and preventive war

The 2003 Iraq war is a benchmark in the escalation of unilateralism by the USA, albeit with the collusion of the UK and a handful of other nations. Former UK representative on the UN Security Council, Sir Crispin Tickell, notes 'The way in which the United States with British support, tried to bully the Security Council into endorsing a war against Iraq, and then, having failed, launched it all the same, is present in all our minds.'[63] He goes on to list other unilateral positions taken by the US: unilateral withdrawal from the Anti Ballistic Missile Treaty; failure to ratify the Biodiversity Convention or to accept the Biosafety Protocol; refusal to join the International Criminal Court; failure to ratify the UN Convention on the Rights of the Child; refusal to accept a new protocol to the Biological and Toxic Weapons Convention.[64] The US is the most prominent non-signatory to the Kyoto Protocol to the United Nations Framework Convention on Climate Change. Professor John Cairns Jnr sees this unilateralism endangering sustainable use of the planet, stimulating larger military expenditures, and undermining multilateralisn in the international system.[65] Its most evident consequence, however, is war.

The Iraq War was justified by the USA as a preventive war, a tenuous claim in the light of subsequent acknowledgement that Iraq did not possess weapons of mass destruction, played no part in the assault on the Twin Towers and was not threatening to attack any foreign state. As Professor John Cairns Jnr points out, preventive war negates the post World War 2 concepts of containment and deterrence.[66] Furthermore, in the case of Iraq, this preventive war was declared to be in breach of the UN charter by the UN Secretary-General, and, therefore, illegal.

Terrorism and the war on terrorism

Terrorism has been a focus of attention in the opening years of the twenty-first century. It is a frightening phenomenon. Professor Paul Wilkinson explains this: 'it is directed at a wider audience or target than the immediate victims. It is one of the earliest forms of psychological warfare … terrorism entails attacks on random and symbolic targets, including civilians, in order to create a climate of extreme fear among a wider group.'[67] He sees terrorism, as practised by all groups rather than simply Al-Quaeda, as both intractable and dangerous. He says of the Israeli-Palestinian and Indian-Pakistan conflicts: 'In both of these cases terrorist attacks could all too swiftly escalate into full-scale wider inter-state war with a significant risk that weapons of mass destruction could be used by the belligerents.'[68]

Imam Dr Abdul Jalil Sajid quietly provides a counter to some of the hysteria which surrounds terrorism: 'Suicide bombers are waging a distinctly modern type of warfare not sanctioned in any faith.'[69]

The hysteria, and the abuses suffered by some Muslims as a consequence, have a source of stimulation in the dramatic proclamation of a war on terror. Our authors give this notion short shrift. 'To "declare war" on terrorists, or even more illiterately, on 'terrorism' is at once to accord them a status and dignity that they seek and which they do not deserve. It confers on them a kind of legitimacy.'[70] Sir Michael Howard goes on to pinpoint the dangerous consequence of this so-called war 'The use of force is no longer seen as a last resort, to be avoided if humanly possible, but as the first, and the sooner it is used the better.'[71] Professor Paul Wilkinson puts it this way: 'it is a dangerous illusion to believe that they can all be eradicated by 'the war on terrorism' or by some simple military or political solution.'[72]

Professor Hew Strachan sees one of the dilemmas of a concept of a war on terror revealed in the debate about how the US treated prisoners in the aftermath of the war in Afghanistan: 'It reaffirmed the readiness of the US to act outside the international framework created by the Hague Convention, the Geneva Protocols, the UN, and the International Criminal Court, which is in the throes of being formed. It decided to treat the prisoners that it had taken not as prisoners of war despite the fact it had declared it was a war.'[73]

Civil war and low intensity conflict

The second half of the twentieth century saw less of war in the form of the armies of sovereign nations' pitched against one another, and more of wars within nations. These were armed rebellions against colonial powers, as in Algeria, civil wars as in former Yugoslavia, and struggles between war-lords in 'failed' states such as Somalia, Rwanda, and Sierra Leone. Professor Martin van Creveld writes of the struggles against colonial powers: 'Each time modern (more or less), heavily armed, regular, state-owned forces tried their hand at the counter-insurgency game, and each time they were defeated.'[74] It is worth noting that the apt term for this type of warfare is asymmetrical. He concludes: 'To sum up, the three hundred year period in which war was associated primarily with the type of political organisation known as the state ... seems to be coming to an end. If the last fifty years or so provide any guide, future wars will be overwhelmingly of the type known, however inaccurately as "low intensity"'.[75] Low intensity is, however, a misnomer in terms of the number of casualties: civil war and asymmetrical warfare may be less misleading. Currently this thesis is enacted before our eyes in Iraq as a superpower with its formidable array of weapons technology finds victory elusive in the face of low intensity warfare.

Deteriorating environments and the competition for natural resources

The competition for scarce resources such as oil, and the use of force to secure them, is our present day reality. Professor Paul Rogers says 'In the past century, the industrialised north has become progressively more dependent on physical resources from the south, as its own deposits of key ore, coal, oil and gas have become progressively more costly to extract. This resource shift has meant that certain physical resources have acquired a strategic significance that, in a number of cases, already results in actual or potential conflict.'[76]

HRH Prince El Hassan bin Talal of Jordan has focused attention on water as one of these scarce resources in many parts of the world, and likely to become more so as a consequence of climate change.[77] No other resource is more fundamental to the survival of all living creatures. Rivers like the Nile, the Mekong, the Danube, supply water to five to ten different states.

Also perceptible is the trend towards unsustainable exploitation of the natural environment as a source of armed conflict. Professor Paul Rogers again: 'the current economic system is not delivering economic justice, and there are now firm indications that it is not environmentally sustainable. This combination of wealth disparities and limits to current forms of economic growth is likely to lead to a crisis of unsatisfied expectations within an increasingly informed global majority of the disempowered.'[78] He sees this response in the form of 'anti-elite movements' which use political, religious, nationalist or ethnic justifications. Professor John Cairns Jnr. expresses it baldly: 'Heniberg (2003) argues that global oil output will peak in 3-12 years. If an aggressive shift toward new energy sources, such as wind, solar, or fuel cells in the mix, is not achieved in the 3-12 year time period, there will be severe, even grim, consequences, such as economic collapse, resource wars, famine, disease, and despotism.'[79]

Poverty and injustice

Professor Frances Stewart's research makes the connection between armed conflict and poverty and injustice. Social groups in a society are unlikely to resort to conflict for cultural reasons alone, 'horizontal inequalities' are likely to be involved. 'Horizontal inequalities have many dimensions – economic (inequalities in access to incomes, employment and assets), political (inequalities in access to political power) and social (inequalities in access to services, including education, health and housing).'[80] She extends the same analysis to the global situation, pointing out the sharp horizontal inequalities between the west and the Muslim world. Furthermore 'There is empirical evidence of more conflict in poorer economies, those that have weak economic growth and low health standards (Nafziger and Auvinen 2000).'[81]

'The UN Millenium Development Goals in the areas of hunger and malnutrition are not being realised. … As against the target of 22 million, hardly 6 million were escaping from the hunger trap each year',[82] according to Professor M.S. Swaminatham. Not only is development assistance inadequate but 'Global trade is becoming free but not fair. There is no level playing field between the rich and poor nations with reference to trade in farm and many non-farm commodities. There is co-existence of unsustainable lifestyles on the part of a billion members of the human family and unacceptable poverty on the part of another billion.'[83]

According to Sir Crispin Tickell 'At present about 20 per cent of the world's people consume between 70 per cent and 80 per cent of its resources. The dividing line between rich and poor is not only between countries but also within them.'[84] Then he delivers the memorable quotation from the UN Secretary-General, assessing progress on the Millennium Development Goals in July 2002

> There is no autopilot, there is no magic of the market place, no rising tide of the global economy that will lift all boats, guaranteeing that all goals will be reached by 2015.

Professor Stephen Castles is also succinct: 'Under-development is not a natural condition of the South, but a process resulting originally from colonialism and now from the North-South division.'[85]

Availability of weapons across the spectrum from small arms to weapons of mass destruction

In his paper for *Preparing for Peace*, Professor Robert Hinde states that two things are necessary for war to take place: weapons, and people to use them.[86] Section 2 of Part One has already described our world awash with weapons across the spectrum from small arms to weapons of mass destruction.

Responses

There are two evident categories of response to these threats: one global and regulatory, the other more local and occupying the space external to government, for which the term 'civil society' is frequently used. This is no simple dichotomy, however, as there is an area of overlapping activity. Within this overlap there is a vital relationship between the two, with the potential for still greater vitality.

Global response

All the six major threats, both direct and indirect, require a global response in order to reduce and ultimately banish them. International law, as expressed in the UN charter, agreements, treaties and conventions, provides an overarching framework. Many of the systems and institutions of international humanitarian law necessary to human security and international stability are already in existence, but require greater commitment from world leaders and governments.

As Dr Javier Solana, Secretary-General of the Council of the EU argues 'if we want multilateralism to work, then the powerful need to put their power behind it. A complex world needs multilateral bodies – but it also needs leadership. If we prefer a future based on mutually beneficial inter-dependence rather than strategic rivalry, then a stronger and more universal attachment to international rules is in all of our long-term interests.'[87] Dr Grossrieder notes that 'The [Geneva] Conventions remain up-to-date in terms of their content, but suffer from a lack of political will to make sure they are applied.'[88] Judge Richard Goldstone similarly argues for wider and better use of existing humanitarian law and for better enforcement: 'If would-be war criminals truly feared arrest and punishment some of them would think twice.'[89]

In addition to upholding existing law, there is a need to expand and improve it. In the wake of the contested legality of the Iraq war, Goldstone suggests that there is 'a growing need for more definition' and 'a need to look at whether international law is coping'.[90] Sir Crispin Tickell highlights an aspect of this

> I was also the witness of the development of new attitudes towards national sovereignty, a political concept first given legal force by the United Nations Charter. So far, respect for

sovereignty has been a foundation stone of the United Nations and its various institutions. … But over the years recognition of the constraints on it has become general, and erosion of the practice if not of the concept of sovereignty is widespread. Generally states are no longer watertight – if they ever were – from international law and practice.'[91]

Law and regulation require institutions for delivery. Foremost among these is the UN. Its uniqueness and importance are acknowledged by all our authors, but with no illusions. As Brian Walker puts it 'It is not a perfect institution – far from it. But it is one of the best tools we have for replacing war by humanitarian law, dialogue, diplomacy and non-violent action.'[92] Sir Crispin Tickell offers his list of priorities for reform

> … the UN system has had almost excessive political credibility. Far more responsibility is loaded on it than it can possibly carry. Secondly, the tasks it is given are often confused or imprecise, not least because member states themselves do not know how to cope with them. Thirdly, it is not given the financial and other resources it needs to function effectively. The reason it did not succeed in Kosovo was that it did not have anything like sufficient resources. Lastly, it is not allowed to carry through necessary internal changes and reforms.[93]

Some would see these ideas as falling short of the radical change required to democratise the UN. An early priority would be to address the fundamental conflict of interest whereby the five permanent members of the Security Council, the body with the highest level of responsibility for regulating peace and war on our planet, are the top five countries profiting from the arms trade. George Monbiot has published an interesting set of proposals for reform, which include an elected Parliament.[94]

We can be encouraged, however, by the UN's own set of proposals for reform in the report 'A more secure world: Our shared responsibility', which include a model involving regional representation on the Security Council.[95] This was followed up in March 2005 by a set of integrated proposals for reform covering development, security and human rights.

The supra-national regional organisations are important in themselves, but also as building blocks in global governance. The EU offers a model for establishing peaceful relationships between nations which had warred for centuries, for economic success, and for the voluntary relinquishing of sovereignties in order to achieve these valuable outcomes. The African Union, the Nordic Group and the Association of South-East Asian Nations are other examples with both potency and potential.

The UN, the regional organisations, and many international NGO's have accumulated expertise in conflict prevention, resolution and transformation. Dr Scilla Elworthy lists some indicators which alert us to 'conflict brewing': denial of rights, theft or diversion of resources, occupation of territory, oppression of a minority, arms build-up, breakdown of the rule of law, militias out of control, increasing power of war-lords, and terror attacks.[96] She goes on to add

> most intervention concentrates on those who have interests in violence, rather than on those who have interests in peace. The Oxford Research Group is currently researching 50 accounts of effective interventions in conflict, interventions using other tools than force. These successful interventions concentrated on supporting those who opposed violence, in various ways.[97]

During the past year, we have seen this sort of process in action in Ukraine.

In her paper 'Leading a UN Mission: Angola 1992-93',[98] Dame Margaret Anstee conveys the political grind and gritty physical realities of peacemaking: we can have no illusions that this work is anything other than hard. The grounds for hope in this account lie in the evidence of the value of professionalism, expertise and learning from experience, in carrying out the work; and Anstee's observations on a return visit nearly a decade later when she learnt that her intervention had been more appreciated than the contemporaneous feedback conveyed, and that the intransigent attitudes by some parties had not been as uniformly held as it appeared at the time. This was confirmation of her own persistence and of the importance of acknowledging every chink of rationality and humanity expressed in conflict torn circumstances.

A high priority requirement is further development of a multinational policing service which would be trained in inter-personal negotiating skills, and minimal use of armed intervention. It is an irony that some armies are evolving in this direction, but the primary and historical function of armies as instruments of aggression as opposed to the police role of restoring status quo, moderates their full effectiveness in these roles. A radical direction for the evolution of military services would be to create a weapon-free sector, in which recruits would never handle weapons but would cultivate these other skills and qualities.

Poverty, trade injustice and environmental damage are all tackled by international institutions. Professor M.S. Swaminatham has some useful suggestions. 'It is high time for UNEP (UN Environment Programme) to be developed into a World Environment Organization, on the lines of the World Trade Organization.'[99]

> It is also necessary to reflect on methods of giving meaning and content to the ethical obligations of scientists in relation to society. The World Conference on Science held at

Budapest in 1999 called for a new social contract between scientists and society. With a rapidly expanding Intellectual Property Rights (IPR) atmosphere in scientific laboratories, the products of scientific inventions may become increasingly exclusive in relation to their availability, with access being limited only to those who can afford to pay.[100]

The case has been made, by major aid organisations like Oxfam and by insiders like Professor Joseph Stiglitz,[101] former chief economist at the World Bank, that some international agencies have been part of the problems that they exist to resolve. The World Bank imposes loan conditions on developing countries which cripple development, and the World Trade Organisation has been successful in opening up markets in the developing world while protecting those in the west. The European Union is guilty in this respect, with its subsidised agriculture undermining agriculture in the developing world. These critics do not conclude that these organisations should be abolished, but they should be reformed to operate rationally and effectively to achieve the objectives of free and fair trade. A case has been made for allowing developing countries selective trade protections while they are establishing.

Nuclear weapons are a crucial object of international regulation. The 1972 anti-Ballistic Missile Treaty limited deployment of nuclear weapons by the USA and the Soviet Union. The lynchpin of multi-lateral nuclear agreements has been the Nuclear Nonproliferation Treaty of 1968 in which the then five nuclear powers, the USA, Soviet Union, UK, France and China agreed not to transfer nuclear weaponry, devices, or other such technology to non-nuclear states. Since then North Korea, India, Pakistan and Israel have become nuclear powers. It is being reviewed during 2005. Fifteen to twenty other nation states are believed to be capable of developing nuclear weapons. The 1996 Comprehensive Test Ban Treaty, which banned nuclear tests has been ratified by many of the forty-four states deemed nuclear capable, the prominent non-signatories being the USA, North Korea, India, Pakistan and China.

The banning of anti-personnel land-mines has been one of the relative successes of international arms control. The context, however, is an international trade in arms worth approximately $30 billion a year, which is largely without global regulation. The EU Code of Conduct on Arms Exports, although welcome, represents a very small ethical dent in this merciless activity.

The response from civil society

Most people in most countries are somewhat detached from the workings of international law and global governance. From time to time, however, these distant institutions and decision-makers attract the media spotlight and the general public receives an instant education before the focus moves on. One such moment was the attention received by the UN Security Council in the run-up to the Iraq war. Another was the logistics of systems for emergency relief in the wake of the 2004 tsunami in the Indian Ocean. Of growing importance is the internet in making the work of global institutions both transparent and accessible. Civil society as enacted by citizens in their cultural activities, educational institutions, clubs, associations, churches, consumer groups, villages, towns, and cities, has been the locus for the formation of ideas and opinions, and for constituting each individual's world view. Modern communications and globalisation have stretched that locus, arguably adding another 'virtual' dimension in the form of the internet. Civil society for many people for much of the time has global dimensions.

Professor Sir Joseph Rotblat makes this comment

> The fantastic progress in communications and transporta-
> tion is transforming the world into an intimately inter-
> connected community, in which all members depend on
> one another for their material well-being and cultural
> fulfilment. More and more people are acquiring the techni-
> cal means, such as the internet, to talk to one another
> wherever they may be. This helps to remove prejudice and
> mistrust which stem mostly from ignorance.[102]

Within civil society the activities which are crucial to the global response to major threats include education, sustainable interaction with the environment, an awareness and a regard for justice in the judicial and economic spheres, faithful practice of religions, maintenance of the fabric of democracy through the peaceful articulation of the interests of all sections of the community.

Our authors have their own take on these themes. Professor Robert Hinde reminds us of the 1974 UNESCO recommendation that member states should foster peace education and monitor the results, noting that that Finland is the only country to have followed this advice.[103] Professor John Cairns Jnr says 'the intent to live sustainably and leave a habitable planet for posterity is the ultimate social contract'.[104] Hinde again: 'parents cannot be expected to bring up children as prosocial and cooperative individuals unless they are themselves living in a reasonably secure environment. That means that a major effort to reduce poverty worldwide is necessary, and that in turn requires the reduction in wealth differentials and a fairer distribution of the Earth's resources.'[105] The common message in the world's religious texts is an exhortation to peace not war; Imam Dr Abdul Jalil Sajid resists the use of Islam to justify terrorism: 'When the Prophet (Peace Be Upon Him) saw the body of a woman casualty of war, he stated, 'She was not fighting. How then came she to be killed?'[106] Dr Paul Grossrieder comments 'When the human cost of war is prominently reported, public opinion intensifies its rejection of violence and strongly insists that it be stopped, and that "something be done". This puts pressure on governments.'[107]

The disintegration of the coercive system of communism in Eastern Europe was brought about partly by dissident groups recognising their impotence in using force or even traditional political methods, and concentrating instead on developing a civil sphere within the regime where human values were esteemed. In *The Unconquerable World*, Jonathan Schell describes how powerfully and peacefully subversive this 'living in truth' proved to be, engaging even the soldiers and police who might otherwise have suppressed its expression.[108]

Leadership

There is a unique connecting relationship between civil society and government, and that is leadership. It is a relationship which can bear the heaviest of formal responsibilities in holding political office, or act as the voice articulating for a given group any feature from the spectrum of human experience. It is an exercise of influence in both directions, the leader over the led, and the led over the leader.

Dr Chris Williams and Yun-Joo Lee give a penetrating and far-reaching analysis of leadership and war. This is how they introduce their paper: '*War is made in the minds of men*, concluded the founders of the UN. But it is made in the minds of particular 'men' – those who are leaders. If the idea of war as a political force is to change, the minds of those with power must change. We cannot make war totally unthinkable. It has been invented, so it will always be thinkable. But how is it is possible to create a context in which war is unthinkable because it is not perceived as a feasible, rational or legitimate political act by those with power?'[109]

They share with Hinde, and others, the concept of war as a social institution, which is, therefore, not an inevitable feature of our lives. Leaders create contexts, link together ideas and feelings, define enemies, in order to motivate people to go to war. Williams and Yun-Joo: 'there is now a broader realisation: contemporary conflicts are not fundamentally caused by phenomena described in popularist terms such as "nationalism", "ethnic hatred" or a "clash of civilizations". Such conflicts are constructed and fuelled by powerful people to serve their own ends.'

On the other hand, they acknowledge: 'War is made by leaders, but so is peace and security, and many other "goods" of life.'[110] In exploring how leaders can make the transition between leadership for peace and leadership for war, they use theories about self-perception, hard and soft relations, and set out a key role for global regions: 'The significant point about the modern regions is their federal nature and plurality of power – no single leader has absolute power. Leaders are part of a regional leadership; they are not regional leaders.'[111] What this paper brings home to us is that not only can we seek to influence the ideas of leaders but we can also seek to shape the very activity of leadership.

In Part One we put forward the case for the irrationality of using war as a political tool in the twenty-first century. In Part Two we have set out the range of tools, other than war, which are available to deal with threats to peace. This has brought us via the discussion on civil society to our own front doors: what part can we play as citizens or as leaders in a world preparing to become a peaceful global community? The next chapter will offer one answer to this question. It will also face more concretely the question which this chapter has probably left in many people's minds about whether the use of force can be avoided when the violence of war is unleashed on a population.

PART THREE

CONCLUSIONS

CONCLUSIONS

The broad thrust of our experts' contributions, taken together, is that war has been rendered redundant and obsolete as a tool for resolving conflict in the twenty-first century. It is an antiquated institution, not functional in the modern world: it causes more problems than it solves. It is surplus to requirements and unnecessary: we have better ways of resolving conflict.

There is a need to relinquish the many illusions built around war. We are told of war being waged in the name of freedom, peace and the spread of democracy. Do we really believe peace and democracy can be brought in the same parcel as a life-long legacy to a generation of children affected by fear, pain, loss, death, homelessness and hunger? Are traumatised adults, or adults angered to their cores by assaults on who and what they love, receptive to the good intentions of their attackers? It is time to open our thinking about war to other reservoirs of knowledge and experience so that we cease to behave with such astonishing irrationality.

Preparing for peace means seeking a different route through today's world; a route to a sustainable future for our children and their successors.

Today's world is one world community. Our world and its inhabitants are functioning as an integrated system. Now humanity has to learn to do so knowingly and deliberately, to extend the frontiers of tentative cooperation, to learn how to act responsibly as citizens of one world, and to live in peace and harmony. We only glimpsed the potential of this vision in 1945. We can move forward more quickly and securely if we so choose, in the twenty-first century.

International efforts to promote rational solutions to collective problems do not founder for lack of knowledge or even lack of expertise most of the time, although the institutionalisation of peacemaking and peacekeeping is still in its infancy. The crucial deficit is political will based upon a morality which understands the imperative of our common humanity. By contrast the ruthless self-interest of the powerful must be removed or circumnavigated.

The focus of the *Preparing for Peace* concern has been to look through the eyes of recognised experts, drawn from a wide range of disciplines and experiences, at the value of armed conflict as a tool of political will in the twenty-first century. War, we conclude, is not a rational act. It is increasingly an out-dated and outmoded tool for our new century. Scientific and technological developments in the engine of war post 1945, in a world in which the parallel forces of globalisation require us to live more closely to one another, renders war, in all its forms, as increasingly self-contradictory and its consequences virtually impossible to control or predict. The idea that modern war cannot and does not work needs to be examined and embraced, we believe, by billions of our fellow human beings if the twenty-first century is to witness the survival and fullest expression of humanity.

However, the morality of destroying life in war has not been our central issue. Quakers are celebrated for their non-violence and their refusal to be party to trying to solve differences through armed conflict. Non-violence has been our testimony from our inception. It is an insight shared, thankfully, by many others, not only by men and women throughout the Christian faith, but way beyond in Buddhism, branches of Hinduism, Jainism, the Bahai's as well as significant numbers of humanists, agnostics, atheists, and indeed, women and men of good will.

As Quakers our peace testimony is central to our faith. We are, therefore, including our own reflections on this question.

Brian Walker, in his lecture, explained that the early Quakers' pacifism was born of pragmatism as well as morality: they survived persecution by assuring their ruler they were not a threat. These two threads are still present. On the one hand is the person who abdicates from any form of violence or coercion. Those people who live among us with such deeply held conviction, gentleness and regard for life are precious indeed. They uphold for us all the pole of non-violence. For others the futility and destructiveness of war are abhorrent, and the wisdom of non-violent or non-coercive problem-solving is apparent, but they may feel that their personal limits in this respect have never been tested and they are not sure if their faith and courage would sustain them to do what they know is right if they were. The application of these beliefs is never easy in modern society. Nonetheless, their application to 'real-politique' is constantly under examination by modern Quakers. Our peace testimony is not a creed, it has no fixed expression, it is the embodiment of successive generations' attempts to live in their world in the light of their faith.

The four members of the *Preparing for Peace* planning group believe in non violence and the peaceful resolution of conflict. This is not the place to detail that traditional work in all its manifestations in a complex and often contradictory world. Being obedient to the spirit which informs our chosen way as Quakers is a discipline which we commend to others, and which leads us to embrace all forms of conflict resolution excepting the resort to armed violence and all that that implies.

At the heart of pacifism and at the heart of all religions is respect for life. It is by leading our lives with close attention to what that means, and maintaining an open mind, that we best determine how we should act in the situations which challenge us most deeply. This still allows for differences of opinion or judgement and different emphases, which is why Brian Walker in his lecture urged that, 'We should not exaggerate the differences between honest Friends.' We may extend this to all honest friends.

Self-evidently the vast majority of people are neither pacifists nor enthusiasts for war. They offer for consideration situations in which, like our speaker General Sir Hugh Beach, they see war as the lesser of two evils, or see no alternative. The time-frame is crucial to any such consideration: just as the circumstances for armed conflict are created over time so may they also be anticipated and mitigated. Two useful strategies not yet highlighted are modelling and exposure. Unfortunately we are witnessing at present a negative version of modelling by some of the most powerful nations, including our own, in that unilateral war-making, human rights abuses surfacing during the 'war on terror', and plans for new types of weaponry including nuclear, biological and chemical weapons, all legitimise similar actions by other nations: the Russians in Chechnya and the Israelis in conflict with Palestinians claim to be waging a similar 'war on terror'. Learning from imitation tends to be more effective than learning from direction. Powerful nations have a duty to model good conduct in international relations, democratic practice and sustainable development.

Similarly naming and exposure of wrongdoing can have considerable force. Repeatedly powerful nations have held back from this strategy because of other less honourable, political calculations. The civil war in the former Yugoslavia was wrongly named as the resurfacing of chronic ethnic conflicts, when it was a deliberate strategy by politicians to exploit those human weaknesses in order to obtain power. We saw at the end of the Cold War and

more recently in Serbia, and the Ukraine, how a population can be supported in upholding the rule of law by an
international community which endeavours to use the
media to tell a truthful story.

Beach's example of General Dallaire's dilemma in
Rwanda[112] is a challenging example for the UN and the
pacifist alike. It may be argued in this case that a model of
intervention closer to a policing operation, and using very
large numbers of personnel who flooded the country with
witnesses, may have prevented the slaughter; while
acknowledging that the evaluation and decision-making in
cases such as these are indisputably difficult.

Our position today is that we know a lot about the causes of violent conflict, a lot about preventing it, and a lot
about responding to it without recourse to war. The politics of the twenty-first century could be built on this
knowledge. The insights delineated by our speakers need
to be considered by billions of our fellow women and men.
That is a challenge of world scale proportions, and some
will try to avoid the challenge on those grounds. But that
is precisely how things must have appeared in the smaller
world when people began to question the morality and
wisdom of slavery as the foundation of economic activity,
or of treating women and children as chattels. The key
point here is to have the courage and wisdom to learn how
to make political decision-making conform to what is truly
in the best interests of our children and grandchildren.
Twenty-first century humanity is at a tipping point when
the degradation of armed conflict can be translated into the
practice of pragmatic, rational and peaceful politics both
nationally and internationally.

It has been noted that in Britain, as well as other
European countries, voter turn-out in elections is dropping. One explanation is that electorates are not offered
policies that measure up to the real political questions of
our times. These questions are the ones with global reach.

Throughout Europe and North America much of our media and most of our politicians strive to keep the focus on the domestic and exaggerate the politics of our public services. We may speculate about why our politicians are inhibited in talking about the importance of international bodies which transcend the nation-state. The European Union, for example, together with China, has the potential to help in containing the hegemony of the USA and to be a greater regulatory influence on global capitalism: hence we may expect negative messages from these vested interests. It is in the regional and international contexts that our national politicians may be challenged and called to account by their peers: small wonder they are ambivalent about these bodies. A new generation of politicians is needed, who are unbound by nationality and the nation-state, who understand today's issues as global issues, and have the courage to lead the way along untrodden paths.

In summary, our conclusion is that war is both redundant and obsolete. That apparently simple idea needs to be seeded in minds throughout the world. There already exist tried and tested methods for resolving conflict. We are advocating, therefore, a programme under three main headings

- The proscription of war under international law
- The creation of new institutions to transform conflict
- Sustained and effective action to eliminate the causes of war.

We also invite leaders to commit to putting this programme into practice by moving step-by-step in the direction of the following policies

- A UN constitutional amendment that war is illegal for any reason.
  This would be coupled with the more rigorous application and development of processes now available in

embryonic form, for dealing with nations or organisations which threaten or make war.

- International law to include a set of reformulated crimes against humanity.
  These will ensure that leaders who prosecute war and violence in response to perceived disputes within or between nation states, should be subjected automatically to the full rigor of international humanitarian law administered through the UN. Such law will need to be developed and refined during the forthcoming decades.

- Reform of the UN to make it a truly representative body. This would build upon the current proposals by the Secretary-General, with an objective of a Security Council giving fair representation to all nations, and the commencement of a programme to democratise the UN with a globally elected parliament.

- Establishment of an international civil peace service. This would build upon the existing components of the civilian peace service, be answerable to the UN and be composed of civil peacemaking and peacekeeping units, some of which would be recruited and trained as multinational services, and some would be seconded units from nations or supra-national regional organisations. The multinational services would include an international police service.

- Development of supra-national regional bodies. In addition to being vehicles for cooperative action by the nations in their membership, these bodies would enable their citizens to realise their roles as global citizens by developing their capacity to uphold a democratically operating UN.

- Control of arms production and trade in arms; decommissioning of weapons of mass destruction.
  This would be in the form of international law, under a UN maintained and controlled register of arms sales, backed up by inspection and penalties for infringement.

- Sustainable development, protection of the environment and trade justice.
  Just as the most progressive nations have passed laws and evolved social institutions to promote equal social and economic opportunities for their citizens, protect vulnerable people, tackle threats and damage to the environment, conserve precious resources, assist poor communities, and generate wealth, so we should act as a global community to discharge our responsibilities for one another.

- Programmes to educate the present generation of the world's children for their future responsibilities as world citizens.

These are the inseparable constituents of making a peaceful world, a world with hope at its heart. We should recognise the futility of war as a tool of modern politics and evolve, as a consequence, rigorous and peaceful methods for settling disputes. We can succeed in this great endeavour by acting henceforth as global citizens of one world. We can seek out global leaders worldwide, irrespective of country, who will take us down this road.

PART FOUR

SUMMARIES OF PAPERS

SUMMARIES OF PAPERS

(Papers are presented in full on www.preparing forpeace.org)

In alphabetical order

Dame Margaret Anstee: 'Leading a UN Mission: Angola 1992-93'
The first woman to head a UN peace-keeping mission with command over military, police and civilian elements, and the first woman to achieve the rank of UN Under Secretary-General, Margaret Anstee describes the political and day-to-day realities of her task in Angola, and the lessons for future planning of similar operations. She undertook the assignment after the signing of the Peace Accords between the MPLA government of Angola and the UNITA rebels. The task was the formation of new joint armed forces from the rival armies and the holding of elections within sixteen months of the signing. Major problems included negotiating for resources from funding nations, persuading reluctant leaders to meet one another, the logistics of running the elections, becoming herself the target of vituperative criticism, with the warfare continuing meanwhile. A visit to Angola in 2001 gave her the opportunity to revise in a favourable direction her own evaluation of the contribution she had made. Her piece concludes with reflections arising from her forty years of service.

Originally published in *Never Learn to Type – a Woman at the United Nations*, John Wiley & Sons, 2003. Reproduced by kind permission of the publisher and writer.

General Sir Hugh Beach: 'Is war successful in achieving its objectives?'

A veteran of the Second World War and former occupant of senior military staff positions, General Sir Hugh Beach is also an Anglican who views war through the moral principles of the Christian Just War doctrine. His thesis is that there are times when war can and must succeed in achieving a humanitarian aim – in reversing a grave public evil, for example. He explores the Just War doctrine in relation to intervention in Kosovo, and analyses also the costs of failing to intervene in Rwanda. However, Beach is realistic about the complexities inherent in conducting a humanitarian war. He looks at questions of right intent, proportionality and civilian immunity, finding that the methods used do not always support the humanitarian aim (e.g. high altitude bombing). He notes that even if military intervention is necessary to bring hostilities to an end, it is only a small part of the answer: the major task is rebuilding the social fabric. His ultimate conclusion is that the military can play a part in achieving a better peace, but that war should always be a last resort when other methods have failed; and it must be used with as much precision as possible.

Sir Samuel Brittan: 'The ethics and economics of the arms trade'

Gifted to **Preparing for Peace** by the author, this paper was originally a lecture delivered to the Royal Society for the encouragement of Arts, Manufactures and Commerce. In it, political economist Sir Samuel Brittan analyses the economic case of the arms trade, focusing on the UK. His central thesis is that the economic support given to the arms trade in the UK cannot be justified on economic grounds. In order to substantiate this claim, Brittan examines each of the most common arguments used to justify the arms trade, including export promotion, employment, terms of trade and spill-over benefits. Brittan also explores what might happen if UK arms exports were cut by a third; the resulting impact on the UK economy would, he argues, be negligible. In conclusion, Brittan does not argue for an outright ban on all arms sales, but rather an effective ban on the sale of arms to dubious regimes, for a complete end to arms export subsidies, and for an authoritative audit of the trade. He suggests, furthermore, that the IMF and World Bank should insist on a curb to spending on military hardware and a limit to small arms exports as a condition for receiving aid.

Professor John Cairns Junior: 'War and Sustainability'
Gifted to *Preparing for Peace* by the author, editor and publisher, this paper first appeared in the *International Journal of Sustainable Development and World Ecology*.

Scientist Professor John Cairns Jnr assesses the impact of war on natural systems and natural capital. His central thesis is that war is an unsustainable activity in a world of finite resources and damaged ecologies. He looks at a variety of factors, including tipping points, risk, distress and security. He concludes that as well as depleting and damaging natural capital, war exacerbates existing problems of poverty, economic collapse and damaged public health systems; moreover, unless sustainable practices are adopted now, we risk more 'resource wars' in the future. Cairns argues that warring parties should aim to limit environmental damage in the way that they currently aim to limit harm to civilians and societal infrastructure. Ultimately, however, he argues that humankind will have to choose between war and a process of transition from unsustainable to sustainable practices. In his opinion, only sustainable use of the planet can provide the global community with real security.

Professor Stephen Castles: 'Environmental change and forced migration'
Gifted to *Preparing for Peace* by the author, this paper was originally a lecture delivered at Green College, Oxford, in December 2001. An expert in migration and refugee studies, Professor Stephen Castles explores forced migration through conflict and through environmental change. In doing so he enters a live debate into what the 'real' causes of forced migration are. Castles concludes that environmental factors should be seen as part of broader processes of societal change, and that factors such as political and ethnic divisions and economic interests are more important as causes of war and violence. His answer is to deal with the root cause of forced migration. He suggests promotion of sustainable development; foreign aid measures to alleviate environmental pressures and assist impoverished groups; relief of foreign debt for the poorest nations; and initiatives designed to help developing countries deal with environmental challenges. By way of conclusion, Castles argues that the international community should not simply associate the developing south with security risks and environmental problems: underdevelopment is not, he claims, a natural condition of the south, but rather a consequence of past colonialism and more recent polarisation of north/south economies and policies.

Professor Lynn Davies: 'Conflict and Chaos: War and Education'
Professor of International Education and Director of the Centre for International Education and Research at the University of Birmingham, Lynn Davies gives a summary of her wider work exploring the links between conflict and education. Given the complex nature of these relationships she commences with an account of complexity theory and conflict, before describing four categories of links. Firstly, she looks at the roots of conflict such as

inequality, ethnicity or gendered violence, and sees where schooling is implicated in such social phenomena. Secondly, she looks at the effects of violent conflict on education itself. Thirdly, at the direct impact of school curricula and organisation on conflict – in war education as well as peace education. Fourthly, at strategic educational responses to conflict – post-conflict reconstruction as well as conflict resolution within the school. Finally, she sets out a vision for the future and how things could be different, using the concept of the 'interruptive school', which can 'interrupt the processes towards more violence'.

Dr Scilla Elworthy: 'How wars could be prevented: Friends' contribution to policy change'
A Quaker and founder of Oxford Research Group, Dr Elworthy provides a practical guide to understanding and influencing political decision-making in respect of war. Though directed primarily towards a Quaker audience, her analysis and advice is applicable to anybody wishing to operate as a global citizen. Her thesis is that change is possible and that there are feasible and effective ways of containing conflict without recourse to war and violence. Elworthy begins by outlining the importance of non-violent preventative strategies and processes of conflict resolution. Looking at the flaws in current thinking, she argues that most resources are allocated to traditional conflict between states; most intervention is directed towards warring factions rather than parties interested in peace; and that most interventions are late. She then explores how decision-making in respect of nuclear weapons emerges from a nexus of politicians, scientists, military strategists, defence contractors, civil servants and foreign office officials; and applies her analysis to the processes behind plans for a US National Missile Defense system. As a conclusion to her paper, Elworthy sets out a number of practical steps through which ordinary people might affect policy.

Judge Richard Goldstone: 'Prosecuting war criminals'
With widespread experience as a judge at war crimes tribunals in The Hague, and in the South African Court of
Truth and Reconciliation, Judge Richard Goldstone assesses the development and impact of international humanitarian law. Beginning with the role of Henry Dunant,
founder of the International Committee of the Red Cross,
he describes the genesis of conventions and treaties in
respect of war, genocide, torture and terrorism; the use of
international jurisdiction; the development of an international criminal court; and the work of war crimes tribunals.
Concerned by political gamesmanship surrounding the
launch of the International Criminal Court, he argues for
greater recognition of the needs of victims. Having compared the cases made for intervention in Kosovo and war
in Iraq, he also argues for greater care in definition.
Ultimately, he believes that war crimes tribunals have been
successful in a number of key ways: they have been fair,
they have advanced the law, and have led to more con-
certed attempts to minimise harm to civilians in war. He
concludes by pointing to the power of public opinion in
limiting the use and effect of war, and the power of individuals such as Henry Dunant, suggesting that every person can make a difference.

Dr Paul Grossrieder: 'The human costs of war'
With the benefit of his experiences as Director General of
the International Committee of the Red Cross, Dr Paul
Grossrieder explores the human costs of war in its widest
sense, describing the impact of conflict on the safety,
health, education and livelihoods of individuals and communities. Using examples from around the world, he
describes sexual violence, displacement, loss of freedom,
lack of access to water and food, abandonment of livestock, health problems, the collapse of education and the
collapse of the family. He notes that perhaps the most

traumatic effect of war is the collapse and dispersal of the family and the psycho-social suffering that ensues. In addition he points to less obvious effects, such as the suffering of poor countries hosting refugees, the suffering of hostage populations, and the stranglehold warring factions might have on a local economy. In answer to the question 'What should be done?', Grossrieder makes key suggestions: a universal movement to tackle the causes of war; use of the power of images through media coverage; serious efforts to protect civilians when war breaks out with due observance of the Geneva Conventions; prevention, including preventative deployment of peacekeepers; and the mobilisation of multinational companies – companies which, he argues, should comply with the principles of international humanitarian law. His ultimate hope is that the global community recognises the horror, suffering and despair inherent in war.

Professor Beatrice Heuser: 'Is war successful in achieving its objects?'
Professor of Strategic Studies at Kings College, London, at the time of her lecture, Beatrice Heuser looks at the success rate in war after 1945 and at a changing strategic context. Examining the historical record, Professor Beatrice Heuser points to the way in which western powers' view of the usefulness of war was affected by the Second World War experience. Unsurprisingly, perhaps, nations that suffered severe defeat in 1945 exhibit little confidence today in the idea of war as a rational or successful tool of politics; but this revolution in thinking in Germany can be contrasted with the philosophy of the victorious Allies. She argues, however, that 1945 was a defining moment for *all* parties. As they took stock of the consequences of total 'conventional' war, they witnessed the arrival of a new nuclear age. She suggests that though the existence of nuclear weapons and possible 'mutually assured

destruction' did not put an end to conventional war, superpowers were hampered in their efforts to achieve outright victories. However, in conclusion Heuser is not greatly optimistic that we will see the end of war: she argues that it is unlikely that the international community will renounce war as tool of politics, primarily because many regimes have no alternative tools of interstate policy-making.

Professor Robert A. Hinde: 'Why are people willing to go to war?'
Behavioural scientist Robert Hinde looks at cultural and behavioural factors that maintain the 'institution of war'. He looks at different levels and aspects, from violence between individuals and between groups, to war between nations; from the role of care-givers in the home, to the role of the military-industrial-scientific complex. Hinde's central thesis is that attitudes towards war and violence come primarily from societal conditions (such as poverty, inequality and availability of weapons) and the cultural context (which includes militaristic language and references). But, he argues, these conditions and contexts are not immutable: our aim must be to help the militaristic nations and peoples of the world become more like the peace-loving nations and peoples. For Hinde, the principle means of undermining the institution of war is through education, through control of the military-industrial-scientific complex, and through the removal of the social conditions which help support war.

Professor Michael Howard: 'War against Terrorism'
Gifted to *Preparing for Peace* by the author, this paper was originally a lecture delivered to the Royal United Services Institute one month after the terrorist attacks of the 11 September 2001. Writing in the immediate aftermath of the attacks, historian Professor Michael Howard questions the

response of the US in their declaration of a 'war' on terrorism. He argues that this creates a war psychosis, in which people expect the military action and conclusive victory of a conventional war. He therefore questions the political imperative of overt military response, arguing rather that anti-terrorism work is really 'a battle for hearts and minds', generally requiring intelligence, covert operations and police-work. He warns, further, that prolongation of the war on terrorism, with the prospect of a war on Iraq (a suggestion rather than a reality in October 2001), will make it an increasingly difficult war to win.

Professor Paul Rogers: 'The environmental costs of war'
According to Professor Paul Rogers, the environmental effects of war are relatively limited compared to human and economic costs. But, he argues, environmental effects of war can be severe and are potentially 'calamitous'. He points to striking examples of regeneration in the natural and built environment (for example, the rebuilding of cities bombed in the Second World War), but also points to war zones, military industrial sites, and weapons testing areas that have remained contaminated or damaged for long periods. He also points to peacetime disasters at Windscale and Chernobyl nuclear installations for an indication of how a nuclear attack might impact on environment and society. Ultimately, however, Roger's critical concern is the role that environmental crises are playing – and will increasingly play – in *causing* conflict. Rogers warns that if the polarisation of economies and resource-use continues, and humans do not reverse their negative impact on the global ecosystem, we risk a 'dystopic' world of anti-elite violence and resource wars. Rogers advocates socio-economic and political change towards a more just and sustainable world order, processes that he suggests require energy and commitment.

Professor Sir Joseph Rotblat: 'The quest for global peace'
Scientist and Nobel Peace Prize winner Professor Joseph
Rotblat provides a powerful statement of his position on
war and peace in the twenty-first century. His central argument is that modern war threatens global human existence
and war must therefore be de-legitimised. We have, he
argues, the need and the means to dismantle the world's
nuclear weapons within a decade. In his argument for the
abolition of war, Rotblat identifies grounds for optimism:
evidence that society is already moving, albeit uncon-
sciously, towards a war-free world. He notes that war
between member nations of the Europe Union is unthinkable, yet they were mortal enemies for centuries. But he
also sees that much work remains to be done: in his view,
current trends towards peace are tenuous and require con-
solidation and substance. He advocates making war illegal, enhancing adherence to international law, strengthen-
ing the UN apparatus for peacekeeping; and educating
people as world citizens. Ultimately, Rotblat asks readers
to see themselves as members of humankind and in consequence remember their humanity.

*Imam Dr Abdul Jalil Sajid: 'Islam and the Ethics of War and
Peace'*
Conscious of the confusion and myths that have abounded
since 11 September 2001, Islamic scholar and political scientist Imam Dr Abdul Jalil Sajid seeks to create a more
accurate and meaningful debate on notions of war and
peace in Islamic tradition. Islam, he states, stands for
world peace and global justice, and stands against aggression and brutality. In the course of his paper he explores
such things as the sanctity of life; Jihad; principles of justice, truth and peace; rights of combatants and non-combatants; early examples of peaceful co-existence between
Muslims non-Muslims; and the relationship between the
principles of Islam and international law. In conclusion, he

calls for a movement towards global ethics and interfaith dialogue, with reverence of life, freedom and justice; the eradication of poverty and dissolution of discrimination; and the protection of the environment for present and future generations.

Dr Javier Solana: 'Effective Multilateralism'

Secretary-General of the Council of the European Union, and High Representative for the Common Foreign and Security Policy, Javier Solana writes briefly and succinctly in support of multilateralism, or 'rules with teeth'. The war in Iraq is a significant part of the context for his comments. He identifies two major challenges facing us today: the 'network threats' of a borderless world, and the problems of transition to economic and political freedoms which a number of countries are undergoing. These challenges can be met only by the stable framework of law and physical security embodying multilateralism. The powerful need to put their power behind it if we want it to work.

Professor Frances Stewart: 'Development and security'

Development economist, Fellow of Somerville College, Oxford, and Director of CRISE, the Centre for Research on Inequality, Human Security and Ethnicity, Professor Stewart reviews the part played by armed conflict in economic and social development, and considers the implications for policies to prevent conflict. The focus is major, organised, political conflict within states. Countries in conflict frequently show regress rather than progress on economic and social indicators. She examines the evidence for cultural explanations of conflict, and concludes that, alone, they are insufficient. She devotes attention to three prominent hypotheses which give economic explanations. These are group motivation and horizontal inequalities, private motivation and failure of the social contract. She looks briefly at political explanations. She finds that each of these explanations applies in some conflicts and more than one in some cases. She then identifies indicators for countries vulnerable to conflict, and outlines policies for prevention. Central to these are addressing horizontal inequalities. She emphasises that the international community needs to take these policies into account in promoting development: heretofore the IMF and World Bank have not done this. Finally Professor Stewart suggests that global horizontal inequalities play a similar role in international conflict.

Professor Hew Strachan: 'Can war be controlled and contained?'
In this paper, military historian Hew Strachan declares himself 'a Clausewitzian', describing war as a political instrument. Strachan uses his historical experience to help understand military and political control and containment of war since Clausewitz's day, looking at changes in what politicians mean by 'war', changes in the application of the law of war, and the changing relationship between armed forces, populations and governments. He explores the ways in which control and containment of war had seemed to be increasing in the post-Cold War climate; and the ways in which these trends seem to be in reverse in a climate of terrorism and a 'war' on terrorism. Strachan concludes that the primary means of controlling and containing war is to build a stronger international community, requiring greater respect for the nation state, for the UN, and for the international criminal court; and requiring legitimacy in responses to security problems.

Professor M.S. Swaminathan: 'Peace Dividend: Pathway to achieving UN Millennium Goals'
Scientist and current Chair of Pugwash (an international scientific organization dedicated to reducing and eliminating the threat posed to humanity by nuclear weapons and war), Professor M.S. Swaminathan, adopts a holistic

approach to the problem of security and the need for peace. He sees the global community at a crossroads, pointing to proliferation of nuclear weapons, conflict between nuclear states, and the increasing division between ethics and science in the pursuit of new weapons of mass destruction; in addition, he argues that socio-economic problems such as HIV/AIDS, hunger, poverty and unemployment are also threatening world peace and security. He asks for a renewed impetus in realising the ideals engendered at the founding of the UN – to end war and hunger and to promote peace, health and literacy – and a serious commitment to realising the UN's Millennium Goals. Among his suggestions are a Global Convention on Human Diversity, control of small arms, criminalisation of the use of nuclear weapons, global programmes for employment and education, a sustainable development force, and debt alleviation for the poorest countries. Informed by the example and philosophy of Mahatma Ghandi, this Indian scientist makes a clear case for greater recognition of the needs of developing countries in a polarised world.

Sir Crispin Tickell: 'The UN and the Future of Global Governance'
Sir Crispin Tickell draws on his experiences as a former British ambassador to the UN to explore the role and future of the UN. Acknowledging that the processes leading to the 2003 Iraq war were damaging to the UN, multilateralism and global governance, he nevertheless shows that the UN has a history of recovery and change. During his time as ambassador he has seen the UN replace patterns of conflict with general cooperation among members, contemplate force in the management of peace and security, recognise the constraints of sovereignty, and create an agenda on points of global concern. Tickell argues that despite UN failures and shortcomings, it is important to

remember its 'uplifting' ideal. In his view, the great strength of the UN is that it symbolises common aspirations. It is, he argues, the only institution through which the international community can organise and promote planetary action on sustainability, climate change and protection of the environment. In addition, he identifies the actions that he feels are priorities for the UN and the global community: we must reconsider how we define wealth, welfare, human progress and development; we must apply the principles of common but differentiated responsibility for global problems; and we must create partnerships at all levels.

Professor Martin van Creveld: 'War: past, present, future'
Military historian Martin van Creveld charts the changing face of war, from 1,000 AD to the present. In doing so he describes changing technologies and political paradigms. He sees the post-1945 nuclear world as a turning point, claiming that we are seeing the demise of large-scale interstate war, and the rise, in its place, of 'low-intensity' warfare, including *intra*state war and violence. His central thesis is that the three hundred years in which war has been related to the state are 'coming to an end'. He suggests that if states are to deal with the changing nature of the threat, their forces will have to relinquish the doctrines and much of the trappings of a regular army – including 'heavy equipment' – and become more like a police force.

BrianW Walker, 'A Quaker's view of twenty-first century war'
A Quaker and former Director-General of Oxfam, Brian Walker explores Friends' long history of peace witness and asks for renewed impetus in their approach to war and peace today. Walker seeks to move beyond familiar debates over absolute and conditional pacifism, looking instead towards the 'pragmatic abolition of war'. His thesis is that war is not a reliable or sustainable tool of

diplomacy in the twenty-first century, and is harmful to efforts to rectify the global problems of our time. He notes that in the course of his work he has found a similar view among *non*-pacifist diplomats, decision-makers and military personnel. Walker advocates non-violent coping solutions in cases of conflict, with a stronger UN and greater recourse to conflict resolution processes and humanitarian law. He concludes with the suggestion that ordinary people have a pioneering role to play in convincing world leaders that war does not work in the twenty-first century: this insight is, he argues, the most important element to take forward from his paper.

Professor Paul Wilkinson: 'Terrorism: Implications for World Peace'

Terrorism expert Professor Wilkinson provides an analysis of concepts and typologies, from nationalist terrorists and ideological terrorists, to state-sponsored and state-supported terrorists. Surveying the effectiveness and motivation of terrorist activity since 1945, he notes that with few exceptions terrorism has an 'abysmal' record in terms of achieving strategic goals, though other instrumental and expressive motivations can be at work. He then turns to look exclusively at the impact of the attacks of 11 September 2001, and at the nature of the threat from al-Qaeda. Concluding that both 'traditional' and 'new' terrorism pose a serious threat to peace and security, he argues that the idea of a simple military or political solution to these many different kinds of terrorism is illusory. He advocates the development of effective and widely-supported processes of conflict resolution and peace-building, and the development of more effective methods of preventing and combating terrorism. Though he does not believe they will eradicate all terrorism, Wilkinson suggests that conflict resolution and diplomacy can help reduce the underlying causes of conflict, and thereby save lives.

Dr Chris Williams and Yun-Joo Lee: 'The minds of leaders: de-linking war and violence'

Experts in the field of leadership studies, Dr Williams and Yun-Joo put the dynamic of leaders and followers at the heart of their paper. Their central thesis is that wars are not between social groups (such as nations, peoples or civilisations) but rather between powerful leaders. Williams and Joo explore the different processes by which leaders 'invent' war through linking and 'de-linking' functions, circumstances and ideas. Their primary conclusion is that we need to create a context in which war is no longer considered a feasible, rational or legitimate tool of politics by those in power. They describe ways in which war can be 'de-linked' from violence, through drawing leaders into processes of regionalisation and cosmopolitanism; and encouraging leaders to think differently about their own persona and role, through 'hard' and 'soft' relations and responses. In conclusion, Williams and Joo note that whilst many leaders are responsible for creating war, progressive leaders in intellectual, religious and political spheres have been responsible for creating the conditions for peace and security. They argue that contemporary leaders need to be similarly convinced of their potential for peace.

PART FIVE

A sample of eight papers

WHY ARE PEOPLE WILLING TO GO TO WAR?

Professor Robert A. Hinde

Paper gifted to Preparing for Peace in 2002

Introduction

The causation of war is never simple. Every war depends on multiple interacting factors that differ from case to case. But two are always essential – weapons, and individuals to use them. These individuals may be paid to go to war, or they may be coerced to do so: more usually they are more or less willing or even eager. Why should people be willing to go to war? For the most part they know that war can be bloody and horrible. They know that they may be killed or mutilated, that they may be subjected to unimaginable agony. And yet they go. Many of them, perhaps the majority of those who have seen action, come away horrified and disillusioned (Brodie, 1990). What is it that causes them to overcome or to forget their knowledge of what the consequences may be? That is the subject of this essay.

Aggression and aggressiveness

It is first necessary to make a distinction between 'aggression' or 'aggressive behaviour' and 'aggressiveness'.

Aggression and aggressive behaviour are descriptive terms referring to actions directed towards harming others, directly or indirectly. Aggressiveness refers to the basic capacity, propensity, or motivation to harm others. Aggressive behaviour may be initiated in a number of ways – primarily by fear or greed, for instance. Aggression is a tool that may be used for many purposes – robbery, greed, revenge, self-assertion, and so on. But it is only rarely that aggressiveness is the sole basis for aggressive actions. The distinction is important in the present context because the way in which we talk about war tends to be confusing. We refer to a nation that invades another as 'aggressive', and we use the same term to describe an individual who intentionally harms another. But that does not mean that there is anything in common between the two situations except that harm is caused. The psychological and physiological mechanisms that cause one individual to strike another have nothing in common with the chains of command in an invading army. The individual combatants show aggressive behaviour, but we shall see later that the extent to which their behaviour is motivated by aggressiveness varies with the sort of conflict in which they are involved.

During the Cold War era, both sides justified their stockpiles of nuclear weapons by arguing that human aggressiveness makes war inevitable. Not only is aggressiveness not a cause of wars, as we shall see, but a false view of human nature is implied. We do indeed all have the capacity to behave aggressively. That people do sometimes harm others is apparent from the daily newspaper reports of violence, murders, muggings and rapes. But such things are reported only because they are not usual. If muggings were common on the street every day, they would not be reported. For most of the time people are sensitive and caring towards others. From the newspapers we get an idea of those evil strangers out there, whereas for the great majority of the time our everyday experience tells us that the whole world is not like that, that we all have the potential to behave with kindness and consideration to others, to be 'prosocial', as well as a potential to be selfish and aggressive (Hinde, 2002). A critical question is, therefore, what makes the balance between prosocial and anti-social behaviour to swing towards the latter?

The development of aggressiveness

Why are some individuals more prone to show aggression than others? Full discussion of this issue would fill many books, but it is sufficient for our present purposes to point to three groups of factors, mutually influencing each other, that affect the balance between prosociality and self-ish assertiveness. First, individuals tend to be less prone to aggression if they have been brought up by one or two caregivers (usually the mother and father) who are sensitively responsive to their needs and exercise firm but reasoned control. Conversely, people who are brought up in a rigid, harsh and insensitive family, or by *laissez-faire* parents, tend to be selfishly assertive and aggressive. These are of course only tendencies, and influences from the peer group and others also play a role, but the nature of the early social environment is probably the most important factor affecting later aggressiveness (Baumrind, 1971).

Second, the balance between prosociality and anti-social tendencies is affected by current circumstances. If things are difficult, if it is hard for individuals to obtain food and other necessities, competitive tendencies, including aggressiveness, become more prominent. As might be expected, parents living under harsh conditions find it less easy to be sensitive caregivers to their children, and may encourage their children to be self-seeking.

The third issue is that people are influenced by the culture in which they are living. Thus in a challenging environment like that experienced by those who pushed out into the American West in the nineteenth century, assertiveness and independence were seen as virtues.

These three factors can reinforce each other: people behave selfishly and assertively in part because they were brought up that way, in part because circumstances force it on them, and in part because such behaviour is esteemed in the culture. Reciprocally, the behaviour of individuals affects the cultural climate: competitive behaviour and aggression create an anti-social atmosphere, kindness and cooperation a prosocial one. Of course, these are crude approximations, and the interacting factors are much more subtle than it is possible to describe here. But in so far as aggressiveness is important in violence and war, its salience amongst individuals is affected by their past and present social and physical environments (Berkowitz, 1993; review, Hinde, 1997).

Violence amongst individuals

Of course, violence between individuals does not depend solely on their aggressiveness. One can distinguish the developmental factors, referred to in the last paragraph, from predisposing and eliciting factors, though the categories overlap. Predisposing factors include other motivations present at the time that utilise aggression as a tool to achieve their goals – perhaps hunger or greed. In addition, a variety of factors reduce the social inhibitions against behaving aggressively – hot and humid conditions, crowding, alcohol, frustration and so on. Aggression may actually be elicited by the sight of the goal object, perhaps food or money, in the possession of another individual, by the availability of a weapon, the nature of the victim, fear and by the lack of factors that usually inhibit it. More rarely, basic aggressiveness is itself sufficient to lead to aggression (Berkowitz, 1993; Feshbach, 1989).

Again, this is but a crude picture, but the important issue is that the occurrence even of aggression between individuals does not depend solely on their aggressiveness, but on many other concomitant factors.

Aggression between groups

For violence to break out between groups, the individuals within each group must cooperate with each other. Thus prosocial as well as anti-social propensities must operate. The psychological principles involved in cooperation within groups have been extensively investigated (Tajfel and Turner, 1986; Turner et al, 1994). Members of a psychological group see themselves, and are likely to be labelled by others, as a group; they tend to see themselves as dependent on each other; and they tend to see themselves as more similar to each other in certain respects than they are to outsiders, and as superior to the latter.

A number of factors contribute to this. All individuals seek confirmation of their attitudes and beliefs, and often this can be obtained only by associating with others who think in the same way. Confirmation can also be obtained by associating with others who are *perceived* to think in the same way, even if they do not. All individuals feel in some degree vulnerable, and association with others perceived as dependable is reassuring. All individuals have some tendency to be wary of strangers, so association with familiar others, or with others perceived to be familiar, is reassuring. If asked to describe oneself, one describes characteristics of the groups to which one belongs as well as one's individual characteristics. And feeling oneself to be part of a group of similar others, one can take pleasure in the achievements of other group members, basking in 'reflected glory' (Tesser, 1988). Thus perceived similarity with others, familiarity with them, interdependence, and bias in favour of one's group can be mutually facilitatory. People therefore tend to associate with groups they perceive positively, and perceive positively groups with which they associate. The more an individual identifies with a group that he perceives positively, the more his or her own self-esteem is enhanced.

In these ways, the nation or political party become part of an individual's identity. When two groups are in conflict, identification with one's own nation or group enhances negative feelings to the other group, especially if it is perceived as a source of frustration or as an enemy. Preservation of the group's resources, or the integrity of its territory, as well as fear for one's own safety, may be seen as reasons for defence – with attack seen as the best means of defence.

When violence is occurring or impending, these factors enhance the involvement of individuals in collective endeavours. Military training often involves harsh conditions to which all members of a group are collectively subjected, and thereby enhances their identification with each other and with the group. Social identity comes to predominate over individual identity, shared values become critical, and actions taken in defence of those values are seen as justified (Turner et al, 1994). Identification with a military unit enables its members to take pride in its achievements, past and present, and that increases their identification with it. In many training situations the formation of individual relationships, 'buddy relationships' is encouraged, and these relationships play a supportive role in combat.

In all of this, the role of leaders must not be underestimated. They may influence group goals, maximise conditions conducive to group integrity, inspire collective action through their behaviour, and promote loyalty by caring for individuals. Leaders may be chosen because they represent group values or share group goals, but they may impart their values and their goals to the group. But leaders may have very diverse motivations – they may become leaders because they are idealistic, or because they are ambitious. It is a goal of military training to minimise such differences and to inculcate loyalty to the group.

In a conflict situation, loyalty and the leader's example are not the only group factors that augment the likelihood of aggression. Just because the individuals share common goals, kudos attaches to those who take steps to achieve that goal. When individuals are poised to attack but are held back by fear or moral scruples, the individual who acts first, who first throws a brick at the police or whatever, gains status amongst his or her peers. Assertiveness in seeking for status helps to trigger aggression.

When aggressive behaviour is used as a tool to achieve a goal, it is likely to cease when that goal is achieved. When a platoon of soldiers captures its objective, it ceases to attack. But in certain circumstances inter-group violence can involve basic aggressiveness, where individuals strive to hurt members of the other group for the sake of hurting or killing. In such a case the suffering of the victim enhances the aggressiveness of the aggressor. Such a situation is favoured by anonymity, for the victim is a non-person and the aggressor escapes personal guilt. Although the genocides in the former Yugoslavia and Rwanda were probably planned at a high level, they involved the reanimation of old ethnic and tribal hatreds, and basic aggressiveness probably played a large part in the behaviour of the actual perpetrators. The situation in the Holocaust was probably different in that individuals were assigned specific tasks in the mass homicide, and were made to feel less responsible for the end result (Bauman, 1989).

It will be apparent the causal bases of aggression between groups may be even more complex than those of individual violence, but it is helpful to think in terms of a multi-dimensional continuum, provided this is seen as only an heuristic device. We may consider briefly tribal violence, ethnic wars like those in the former Yugoslavia and Rwanda, and the two world wars.

Violence between small tribal groups is often ritualised in a manner that reduces the number of casualties, but the combatants may be inspired to violence by the hope of capturing cattle or women or by the desire for revenge. No doubt loyalty and duty to the group plays some part, and the desire to enhance their status among their peers also plays a role. Dancing, ritual or drugs may help in increasing their motivation or decreasing their fear. But aggressive behaviour is primarily a tool to obtain their goals, and aggressiveness is not the prime cause of the violence.

The wars in Yugoslavia and Rwanda were in some ways intermediate between the conventionalised picture of tribal war given above and major international wars. They involved cultural groups that had previously lived apparently amicably together. There was considerable central control that was made effective by propaganda that played on the cultural differences and provided the combatants of each group with an incentive and an apparent duty to attack each other. The war in Bosnia-Herzegovina was initially a matter of territorial conquest controlled from above, but escalated to extreme levels of brutality. The brutality often seemed to be perpetrated at the whim of local leaders or groups, though they later claimed that they were constrained by circumstances or by orders from above. The aim was to humiliate, terrorise and kill the enemy population in order to remove it from the territory. Similarly in Rwanda the combatants initially saw the conflict in ethnic, cultural, political or idealistic terms, and perhaps fought as a matter of duty, but this led to the arousal of individual aggressiveness, and in many cases killing for the sake of killing seems to have taken over. Thus in the context of war individuals who had previously lived together amicably came to show callous violence. But it was *the war that caused the aggression, and not vice versa*.

Major international wars

We are concerned here with wars that differ, though only in degree, from those just discussed, in three ways. On each side the role of leaders, operating through a hierarchical system, is paramount. Each side is complex, involving many overlapping groups, so that any negotiations must take place between large bureaucracies representing diverse interests. Third, and most importantly, international wars involve a major degree of role differentiation, and war is best seen as an institution with a large number of constituent roles.

This third point is crucial for understanding the motivation of those involved, and requires a word of explanation. In our society, marriage is an institution with two constituent roles, husband and wife. Certain rights and certain duties are associated with each role. At a more complex level, parliament is an institution, with a considerable number of constituent roles – most obviously prime minister, ministers, the members of parliament, and the voting public. The incumbents of each of these roles have certain rights, and also certain duties. Thus the prime minister must chair Cabinet meetings, play a major part in deciding policy, and so on. For the public, casting their votes is both a right and a duty.

In the same way, war must be seen as an institution with many constituent roles – generals, officers, other combatants, munition workers, transport workers, doctors, nurses, air raid wardens, and so on. The incumbents of each role have specific rights and duties, and they do what they do primarily because it is their duty to do so. Thus the munition workers make ammunition because it is their duty to do so, the transport workers take the weapons to the combatants because that is their duty, and the infantry-man moves forwards and tries to kill enemy soldiers because it is his duty to do so. The tank or bomber crew is not inspired by a desire to kill, kill, kill, but rather to do what they have been told is their duty (Hinde, 1997).

Of course that is not all that is involved. Inhibitions against aggression must be overcome: often only quite a small proportion of the infantrymen involved in combat actually use their weapons (Marshall, 1947). There may be times when defensive aggression takes over – when it is nec-essary to kill or be killed. Fear may either inhibit or augment aggression, depending on the situation. Assertiveness, the desire for recognition and status, is sometimes important. The various factors involved in the dynamics of groups are nearly always basic, with loyalty to the leader, group or an ideal playing an important part. More rarely there are times when basic aggressiveness becomes predominant, and the object is to kill rather than to gain any military objective. Such occasions may escalate from fear or the desire for revenge: especially where they involve civilians, as at My Lai, the aggressiveness is not usually condoned (Dower, 1986). The alienation from civilian life inherent in military training may cause the combatant to disregard values that would previously have been central to him or her. But the main factors in the violence are the duties that the institution of war imposes on the combatants. The munition and trans-port workers, equally important in the prosecution of the war, have duties that do not require them to behave aggres-sively, but the duty of the combatants is to fight.

The duty to fight and to kill enemies is not the only way in which war exacerbates aggression. War legitimates killing. The bomber crew feels that it is all right to do what they are doing because it is their duty. The soldier who would scarcely hurt a fly when at home can use a bayonet to impale an enemy. Indeed the training for hand-to-hand combat is designed to enhance aggressiveness and to see killing as success. Perhaps for that reason, murders tend to increase in frequency after wars are over.

It is, of course, the case that the other sources of motivation discussed earlier in this essay play a part in the aggressive behaviour of the soldier. But duty is nearly always paramount, and in using the distance weapons that predominate in modern warfare it is the combatant's duty in the institution of war that predominates. That combatants do their duty may also be ensured by military discipline, or by loyalty to buddies, leaders, the unit, country or cause, but the duty imposed by their roles in the institution of war is primary. War causes aggression: aggressiveness does not cause wars.

How can war be abolished?

Wars are diverse. Every war occurs because of a different but complex network of interacting factors. Inequalities, and especially inequalities in resources seen as necessary or as human rights, are important in the causation of many wars. Even in the absence of the threat of war, it is morally important that such inequalities be minimised. If poverty, and the environmental degradation that often enhances poverty, were to be abolished, wars would certainly become less frequent. If the concept of state sovereignty were to lose its place, and to be replaced by a federation under the governance of a world authority, war could perhaps be abolished. But these goals are still distant, and there is no simple prescription for the abolition of war (Hinde & Rotblat, 2000). There seem to be three routes that are often followed.

First, conflict resolution has become a sophisticated branch of social science, and a great deal is known about how conflicting interests can be reconciled. The United Nations and its agencies, as well as religious and secular organisations, have had a number of successes. However the diversity of wars, and the complexity of their causal bases, means that preventing violence between two parties with important but conflicting interests is often going to fail. Attempts to resolve conflicts seldom start before the conflict is intense, and that may be too late. Disentangling the deeply held views of the several parties involved, views whose origins may extend back into past centuries, is nearly always a formidable task, and may be impossible. In any case, the best solution for all concerned may not correspond to some sort of compromise between the views of the leaders involved in the negotiations. This does not mean that attempts to resolve conflicts should be abandoned, but rather that they should be started as early as possible, and not be seen as a panacea.

A second possibility is pacifism. Pacifists who maintain their positions against popular opinion, often suffering in consequence, deserve admiration. That sort of integrity is becoming all too scarce. However it is unlikely that the ideology of pacifism will be adequate to stem the dogs of war. There are likely always to be some who feel that it is sometimes right to fight, however horrible war may be. Limited war may prevent widespread devastation, and even a few who were not pacifists might be enough for war to be waged. Now that war has become so technically sophisticated, the massed armies essential in World War 1 may no longer be needed: it takes only a small proportion of the population to exploit the potential of modern weapons.

But this does not mean that the pacifist has no role to play. In the first place, the more individuals are seen to have integrity, the more hope there is of a peaceful society.

More importantly, in negotiations that attempt to resolve conflicts before violence starts or when peace has been achieved, the wisdom of those who have stood outside the conflict may have an important role. For this two things are necessary. First, they must have achieved respect through endeavours unrelated to the concerns of the two parties in conflict. Second, they must understand fully the political realities of the situation.

A third possibility is to disempower the institution of war by removing the forces that sustain it. This is discussed in the next section.

Undermining the institution of war

We have seen that two things are essential for waging wars – weapons to fight them with and individuals ready to use those weapons. This essay is concerned with the latter. We have seen that the most important factor enhancing the willingness of individuals to go to fight in international wars is the duty imposed by the institution of war. Their sense of duty is usually reinforced by propaganda. In this section, therefore, we examine how the institution of war can be undermined (Hinde, 1997).

Institutions do not simply exist. They must be continuously supported and maintained. The forces that do so may be internal to their structure or external to them or both. For instance, the institution of parliament is embedded in the (unwritten) Constitution of the country, and is supported continuously by the actions of the incumbents of its several roles. If the institution of war is to be undermined, the factors that support it must be neutralised. It is convenient to examine them in three categories.

Everyday factors. Many of the phrases we use in everyday life have military associations. Phrases like 'keeping your head down' and 'digging in' have military origins:

their use in ordinary conversation sanitises their significance in war. Reports on war use euphemisms for the horrors involved: bombing attacks are referred to as 'surgical strikes', the dead as 'the fallen', civilian casualties as 'collateral damage' (Fussell, 1975; Mosse, 1990). Military metaphors are even given respectability in such unfortunate phrases as 'war on want' and 'fighting for peace'. The way in which we think is influenced in part by the language that we use and, although the issue may seem trivial, the use of such phrases helps to give war a respectable image, and its occurrence as an acceptable possibility. The rejection of such 'warisms' could contribute, albeit in a small way, to reducing the power of the institution of war, just as the elimination of sexisms has contributed to greater equality between the sexes.

Many, but not all, films and books about war give it a positive image. It is depicted as the scene for manly virtues – courage, stoicism, fortitude – in an atmosphere of glory, excitement and new surroundings. The focus is on the victors, while the defeated are merely cardboard figures. Death is sanitised, lacking the terror and agony that often precedes it. *All quiet on the Western* Front was an honourable exception, and some of the films made about and since the Vietnam War have tried to portray the real thing. But it is difficult for the film makers to get it right: the portrayal of violence can numb the senses, while concealing the horrors sanitises war. No film or book can capture the intensity or horror of combat for the reader in an armchair.

The fascination of mechanical devices for boys is exploited by the manufacturers of war toys. Such toys tend to make war seem like a harmless game, and as a part of normal life for grown-ups. Battles are re-enacted with toy soldiers, and board games are often based on militaristic themes. Some schools encourage 'war games', trivialising the horrors of war. Computer games, often involving extreme though make-believe violence, are a growing problem.

History has often been taught as a history of wars and battles, supporting a picture of the world as composed of competing groups. The image of the warrior hero is reinforced. Educational radio and television programmes discussing war have taken the position of the politicians and generals. There is much to be done in acquainting children with the nature of war as seen by those involved.

Educators have paid little attention to the 1974 UNESCO recommendation that member states should strengthen the contribution of peace education to international understanding and cooperation, to the establishment of social justice, and to the eradication of the misconceptions and prejudices that hinder these aims. The recommendation was coupled with the suggestion that teachers should be trained to foster these aims and that the results should be monitored. Practically the only country that has seemed to take any serious notice of this recommendation has been Finland. More recently some UK schools have tried to teach children what war really means, and some have even organised trips to the battlegrounds of northern France. The Peace Education Network of the British National Peace Council has taken steps to foster these aims. Some educational systems discuss cultural and religious difference in a way that can augment understanding and reduce antipathy to strangeness, but more emphasis could be placed on the theme of common humanity. And education should be extended to include the characteristics of good governance, and to the nature of the national and international organisations that try to provide it. The nature of non-governmental organisations, and of the United Nations Agencies, are obscure to most people – yet in a democratic world everyone should be familiar with the roles that they play, and have views on how their business should be conducted. Of course there is the danger that educators will believe that they are right, so that a too rigid framework is presented to children. What is needed is an education that encourages thoughtfulness.

But education as normally understood starts only when children go to school. More fundamental are the personalities that children bring to school – and though later influences may be important, personalities are initially formed in earlier life. Here, as we have seen, the role of parents and the early social environment, the nuclear or extended family, is paramount. Children have the potentialities for both selfish assertiveness and aggression, and for cooperation and prosociality: early socialisation can swing the balance either way. To achieve that, in many cases education must start with the education of parents, because there is a strong tendency for parents to believe that the way in which they were brought up is the right way to bring up children. And for education to be effective, parents must be delivered from poverty and inequalities must be reduced.

Here, then, is perhaps the most fundamental issue – the socialisation and education of the coming generation.

Pervasive cultural factors. Closely related to these everyday factors are cultural or societal characteristics that affect the attitudes of individuals to war. In the first place, there are differences between countries in attitudes to war. Some countries are militaristic, some are peace-loving. Such traditions are important since not only can they influence high-level decisions, but also they are incorporated into the self-concepts of individuals, who see themselves as having some of the characteristics of their country. But a country's traditions can change. Over the years Sweden has changed from being militaristic to being peace-loving, and Japan changed in the opposite direction.

Second, national attitudes are often related to myths about the country's or group's past. For instance, colonial wars have been justified by an image of the local population as being intrinsically violent and barbarous, while the conquerors, who had invaded the country and had triumphed because they had the more destructive weapons, were presented as intrinsically peaceful. Anti-colonialists have used a reciprocal image to justify bloody rebellion.

Third, we have seen that how individuals see them-selves is influenced by how they see the group to which they belong. One identifies with the groups to which one belongs, the more so if, as is usually the case, one sees them as better than others. Even in the face of contrary evidence, one sees one's family, church and football team as better than others, or at least better than they really are. These tendencies are exploited in propaganda. Conflict and war necessarily involve distinctions between 'Them' and 'Us', and leaders or governments try to accentuate individuals' perceptions of those differences. And in so far as one iden-tifies with one's own group, one sees a threat to the group as a threat to oneself.

The principal tools of such propaganda are ethnicity and religion, and nationalism. Often ethnic or religious rivalries passed down through the generations are exploited by lead-ers or governments to foment hatred in a manner that will serve the current cause. The potency of ethnic differences has been sadly illustrated by the war and massacres in Rwanda. However the differences are often more perceived than real. Ethnic differences may be perceived by those involved, and presented to outsiders, as natural and immutable. So immutable, in fact that new information is twisted to fit with the stereotyped preconceptions. But in many cases the characteristics on which the groups are seen to differ have little to do with what the conflict is about, hav-ing been reconstructed and exaggerated for political pur-poses. The differences between Tutsis and Hutus had been formalised and exacerbated by the former Belgian colonial administration, apparently on a divide and rule principle. In Yugoslavia the members of the different 'ethnic' groups had been living peacefully side by side, but rivalry between the republics was accompanied by increasingly vehement ethnic propaganda. Such propaganda techniques help to make the cause seem just, so that it becomes the citizens' duty to fight or to contribute to the war effort. Often the rivalries between conflicting groups go back many generations to supposed injustices that must be revenged. The pain caused to past generations is carried forward to the present day by the 'cross-generational transference of pain'. The conflict between Greece and Turkey in Cyprus has been exacerbated by conflicting portrayals of history in the school books and museums, so that past humiliations are seen as needing revenge today (Papadakis, 1995).

Religious differences have also been used to justify war. According to some interpretations of the Qu'ran, it is a duty to kill non-believers. The Old Testament also carries many exhortations to violence. The Crusades were primarily religious wars, though they acquired imperialist and economic aspects. Of the several aspects of religious systems, differences in beliefs are most prone to cause conflict (Hinde, 1999). Differences in ritual or religious experience seem less potent except in so far as they reflect religious beliefs, and moral codes have certain similarities across most religions. As with differences in ethnicity, religious differences are often additional to the basic causes of the conflict, and are exploited to augment the perception of differences. Thus the conflict in Northern Ireland had economic roots, the Catholics being underprivileged, but religion has provided a more obvious mark of difference.

Religious beliefs have also served to help the combatants to overcome inhibitions against killing, and to comfort the bereaved. The imagery of sacrifice was used by both sides in the Second World War, Christ's sacrifice on the cross being associated with death in battle. In World War 1 this was made explicit with a poster showing Christ on the cross and at his feet a dead soldier with a nicely sanitised bullet hole in his forehead (Sykes, 1991).

The effectiveness of such propaganda depends on chan-nelling national or ethnic pride and traditions, religious beliefs and the demands of the situation to serve the current cause by the use of psychological characteristics common to all people. It is helpful here to distinguish between 'patriotism', involving love of one's country, and 'nationalism', implying a feeling of superiority and need for power over outsiders. An experimental approach used in the USA during the Cold War era showed that these two attitudes, though correlated, could be distinguished.

At that time individuals high on nationalism were more willing to use nuclear weapons on the enemies of the USA, but less willing to risk their own lives for their country, than those high on patriotism (Feshbach, 1989)..

Nationalism tends to be self-perpetuating in that the more power a nation has, the more its members see it as spe-cial, the more they tend to protect their own interests, and the less they care about the welfare of others. It thus tends to be exacerbated by the competitiveness of capitalism. It is associated with high values placed on military power, dom-inance, economic opportunity and international competi-tion, with a devil-take-the-hindmost attitude. It thus seems that excessive nationalism is not conducive to a peaceful world. Patriotism, on the other hand, is to be encouraged. Local cultures should be valued and preserved: no one wants to live in a uniform Coca-Cola world.

Both nationalism and patriotism are founded on basic human propensities – fear of strangers, group loyalties, and so on. They are stimulated by propaganda, especially in time of war or of impending war. Parades and cere-monies, saluting the flag and playing the national anthem enhance love of one's country, but may at the same time invite comparison with, and thus denigration of, others. Patriotism is augmented by the perception of the country as the 'mother country' or 'fatherland', and by the percep-tion of fellow-countrymen as kin (brothers-in-arms). It can thus be seen as parasitic on the biological propensity to act cooperatively and prosocially with kin. Propaganda augments nationalism by portraying the enemy as evil, dangerous, and even sub-human: such images depend on the group processes referred to earlier, on the tendencies to fear strangers and to defend oneself.

The military-industrial-scientific complex. President Eisenhower pointed out that the very existence of the military, and the industry that supported it, enhanced the probability of war (Eisenhower, 1961). Some scientific endeavours should not be exempt here, this trio of organisations being perhaps the most important force supporting the institution of war. Each member of the trio can be seen as itself an institution, consisting of a number of sub-institutions, each with its own constituent roles. The nature of the military-industrial-scientific complex differs greatly between countries, and in some it is portrayed as having a primarily peacekeeping role.

The complex tends to have great stability: for instance NATO responded to the end of the Cold War not by seeing its task as accomplished but by extending its perceived sphere of responsibilities. This stability is supported by both external and internal forces. Externally, citizens perceive the complex as necessary for their security, in part because war is seen by many as an inevitable consequence of human nature. (The falsity of this view was portrayed by the 1986 Seville Declaration, disseminated by UNESCO). Politicians allow their reputations to be associated with the country's military strength, and there are close links between arms industries and others with more peaceful goals. The arms industries are seen by members of the public as essential to the economy.

In addition the three members of the complex support each other. This is ensured by the time necessary for the development of new weapons. Each nation seeks to deploy weapons superior to those of its competitors. Scientists are employed to devise such weapons. The military request better and better weapons, and must approve the products. Development is long, costly and risky, so that governments are obliged to offer special terms to the arms industries. Development costs are partly covered by selling arms to other countries. Secrecy is involved at each stage, and the accountability of governments thereby diminished (Elworthy,1991). .

There are also internal forces contributing to the stability of each member of the trio. A major issue is, of course, the career ambitions of the incumbents of the roles in each institution. In addition, each institution has its own regulative processes. The military functions within a set of accepted rules, and is empowered by the use of symbols that authenticate its existence. Military procedures are such as to legitimate the institution itself, and the hierarchical nature of the armed services ensures that it is in the interests of the leaders at each level to maintain the system. Patriotism and loyalty are inculcated by tradition. Scientists and industrialists similarly adopt frames of reference that legitimate their activities. While many members of the three arms of the complex genuinely believe that what they are doing is for the good of humankind, or at least of their country, others employ stratagems to conceal what they are doing from others, and even from themselves. For instance one arms dealer called his business 'Intercontinental Technology' and masked his activities with the claim that he was satisfying 'consumer needs'. He admitted that he deliberately avoided thinking about the human consequences of his trade.

Conclusions

Every war is the result of a network of interacting causes. One way to reduce the incidence of war would be to identify the causes common to many wars, and to eliminate them. That this would be a task of incredible difficulty does not mean that it should not be pursued: a reduction in one or more of the causal factors could reduce the probability of armed conflict. But it is claimed here that two factors are essential, arms to fight with, and individuals willing to wield them, and the focus has been on the latter. How can people's willingness to go to war be removed?

The first emphasis must be on education: education first of parents, so that children grow up with prosocial values, with low aggressiveness, and an ability to sift the wheat from the chaff in government propaganda. But parents cannot be expected to bring up children as prosocial and cooperative individuals unless they are themselves living in a reasonably secure environment. That means that a major effort to reduce poverty worldwide is necessary, and that in turn requires the reduction in wealth differentials and a fairer distribution of the Earth's resources. At the same time this would remove some of the factors that predispose individuals to violence and that trigger and justify its use.

At the group level, attachment to one's own group is an almost essential component of group living, and is a product of basic aspects of human nature. But loyalty to one's own group can be at least partially decoupled from the tendency to denigrate others. Three issues could profitably be considered here. First, socialisation and education can foster understanding of and tolerance for the beliefs and customs of others. Second, efforts must be made to reduce differences between groups with potential rivalries: an obvious issue is the danger posed by single-faith schools. And third, competition between groups could be reduced by a more equitable distribution of resources.

At the international level, efforts must be made to discourage nationalism without diminishing patriotism. This requires policies similar to those mentioned in the previous paragraph. But, even more importantly, the power of the military-industrial-scientific complex must be diminished. This does not necessarily mean immediate and total demilitarisation, for the need for defence and for collective action may remain for many years to come. But support for the complex in the general population could be diminished by a growing realisation that war does not stem from human aggressiveness and is not inevitable. Peace education could help here, and education encouraging independence of thought would diminish the power of propaganda. Industrial conversion from arms manufacture to more peaceful purposes has proved difficult but should not be impossible. Efforts are already being made by the Pugwash organisation to discourage young scientists from entering arms industries, though the distinction from firms with solely peaceful purposes is often difficult to make. Finally, the Achilles heel of the complex is probably the arms trade. As noted above, arms-producing industries depend on sales to foreign countries to reduce their development costs, and those sales make possible violent war between their customers. Stricter and international control over the arms trade would be an enormously important step (Broszka, 1995; Elworthy, 1991).

It will be seen that discouraging people from going to war requires action of many kinds. But the underlying theme that unites them all has seldom been better phrased than in the Russell-Einstein manifesto which led to the formation of the Pugwash movement:

'Remember your humanity, and forget the rest'

Bibliography

Bauman, Z., *Modernity and the Holocaust* (Cambridge: Polity Press, 1989)

Baumrind, D., *Current patterns of parental authority, Developmental Psychology Monographs*, 4, 1 & 2, (1971)

Berkowitz, L., *Aggression* (New York: McGraw-Hill, 1993)

Brodie, M. (ed.), *A world worth fighting for* (East Wittering, W. Sussex: Gooday, 1990)

Brzoska, M., 'The arms trade' in R.A. Hinde and H. Watson (eds.), *War: a cruel necessity?*, pp. (London: Tauris, 1995) pp. 224-37

Dower, J.W., *War without mercy* (London: Faber & Faber, 1986)

Eisenhower, D.D., Public papers of the Presidents of the United States of America. Dwight D. Eisenhower, 1960-1961 (Washington DC, 1961)

Elworthy, S., 'Defence decision-making and accountability' in R.A. Hinde (ed.) *The institution of war* (Basingstoke: Macmillan, 1991) pp. 192-228

Feshbach, S., 'The bases and development of individual aggression' in J. Groebel and R.A. Hinde (eds.), *Aggression and War* (Cambridge: Cambridge University Press, 1989) pp. 78-90

Fussell, P., *The Great War and modern memory* (London: Oxford University Press, 1975)

Hinde, R.A. 'War: some psychological causes and consequences'. *Interdisciplinary Science Reviews*, 22, 229-45 (1997)

Hinde, R.A., *Why gods persist* (London: Routledge, 1999)

Hinde, R.A. and J. Rotblat, 'Eliminating the causes of war'. *Pugwash Occasional Papers*, 2, 3 (2000)

Hinde, R.A., *Why good is good* (London: Routledge, 2002)

Marshall, S.L.A., *Men against fire* (New York: Morrow, 1947)

Mosse, G.L., *Fallen soldiers* (New York: Oxford University Press, 1990)

Papadakis, Y., 'Nationalist imaginings of war in Cyprus' in R.A. Hinde and H. Watson (eds.), *War: a cruel necessity?* (London: Tauris, 1995) pp. 54-67

Sykes, S., 'Sacrifice and the ideology of war' in R.A. Hinde (ed.), *The institution of war* (London: Macmillan, 1991)

Tajfel, H. and J. Turner, 'The social identity theory of inter-group behaviour' in S. Worschel and W.G. Austin (eds.), *Psychology of intergroup relationships* (Chicago, Ill: Nelson, 1986), pp. 7-24

Tesser, A., 'Towards a self-evaluation model of social behavior. Advances in Experimental Social Psychology', 21, 181-228 (Orlando Academic Press, 1988)

Turner, J.C., Oakes, P.J., Haslam, S.A. and C. McGarty, 'Self and collective: cognition and social context'. *Personality and Social Psychology Bulletin*, 20, 454-463 (1994)

IS WAR SUCCESSFUL IN ACHIEVING ITS OBJECTIVES?

General Sir Hugh Beach

Lecture delivered on 14th July 2001

Let us start by putting together two well known aphorisms. The first is from Karl von Clausewitz in his book *On War* (Berlin: Dummlers Verlag, 1832 – English translation by Col. J.J. Graham, London: N. Trubner, 1893) written in the aftermath of the Napoleonic wars. '*Der Krieg ist nichts als eine Forsetzung der politischen Verkehrs mit Einmischung anderer Mittel.*' That is to say – 'war is nothing but the continuation of political traffic with an admixture of other means'. The second is from Basil Liddell Hart, written after World War 1: 'The aim in war is to achieve a better peace' (*Strategy*, Second Revised Edition, Meridian/Penguin Books, New York, 1954, 1967).

These make it clear that war is the interruption of an otherwise peaceful process of struggle, engaged in because those who start it believe they will emerge at the end in a better position politically than they would have been if they had stayed within the normal domain of politics. This domain includes, of course, not only voting and elections and the contest in parliament and press, but also economic and political pressure exerted on other countries or groups in the pursuit of political ends. Those who go to war think they can do better than this. Their ends may be good or bad and often they miscalculate. We have seen both in Germany in the late 1930s and in Serbia in the 1990s how a man can gather to himself dictatorial powers, through the democratic process, and then use them to pursue a war policy that brings his country to the brink of ruin. Quite clearly in such cases the wars, so far from achieving their objectives, produced a peace that was catastrophically worse than the continuation of political traffic would have been. So perhaps we can re-phrase the question along the lines of '*Can* war be successful in achieving its objectives?' The answer, I believe, is that war is usually not successful in this way (because at the end of it *all* participants are worse off than they would have been if the war had not taken place) but that it can be successful, at least in the sense of being the lesser of two evils. I am aware that some thinkers believe this notion of 'the lesser of two evils' is logically incoherent and inadmissible. But I suggest that the price of taking an absolutist, pacifist position should be paid only by the pacifist. In today's world the price of such policies is often paid by innocent, civilian parties. A military man must choose the best among bad courses, but not be shy of saying that he does so on clear moral grounds. I will come back to this in a moment. Meanwhile it may be useful to distinguish some general categories.

The most straightforward, it seems to me, is war as *self-defence*. In 1980, almost as soon as he had seized power in Iraq, Saddam Hussein started a war against Iran. In 1985-87 fighting intensified with heavy loss of life. In 1988 a ceasefire was declared and in 1990 a peace treaty favouring Iran was agreed. It seems to me quite certain that had Iran not defended herself – albeit at great cost – her situation politically would have been far worse as the vassal of Saddam. In moral terms almost everyone agrees that a country has a right to defend itself against unprovoked aggression and clearly sometimes this defence is successful in achieving its objectives.

A generation earlier, in 1958, the then King Faisal of Iraq was assassinated, a military coup brought in a left-wing government under a man called Kassem, Iraq left the Baghdad Pact and almost at once started to make threatening noises against its neighbour Kuwait. The British government, then responsible for Kuwait, pre-positioned an infantry battalion in Bahrain, a planning headquarters in Aden, an air-portable infantry brigade in Kenya (I was on its staff in Nairobi) and a parachute battalion in Cyprus. In 1961, Kuwait was given full independence from Britain with Shaikh al-Salem al-Sabah as Emir. Almost at once Kassem started to move his tanks up to the border. The British deployment plan went into action (by agreement of the Emir, of course) and we put strong forces into north Kuwait along the Mutla Ridge. They were bombed up and fully ready to fight. This was enough and as a result not a shot was fired. Kassem called off his tanks. The British were soon able to go home. Kuwait enjoyed thirty years of peace. This was military action as *deterrence*. It was in dismal contrast to the weak line taken by the American ambassador April Glaspie in August 1990 which led Saddam to assume that this time he could get away with overrunning Kuwait. (Some of you may wish to point out that the west had been supporting Iraq during their war with Iran, thinking the latter to be the worse of the two. The enemy of my enemy is my friend. It was indeed a disastrous miscalculation but does not affect my argument.) As a deterrent military action can be successful. Diplomatic pressure unsupported by any sign of military commitment can spectacularly fail. So, *pace* Scilla Elworthy (*Preparing for Peace* author of the paper 'How wars could be prevented: Friends' contribution to policy change'), do not let us get too far carried away by the notion of non-violent conflict resolution as a panacea.

A third category, and perhaps the most topical, is war as *humanitarian intervention*. Is this ever justifiable and under what circumstances can it succeed? I spoke just now of a 'successful' war in terms of the lesser of two evils. Let me now amplify this by rehearsing the views of Christian thinkers under the rubric of the 'Just War'. The two most prominent, Augustine of Hippo and Thomas Aquinas, were philosophers of the first rank who took their stance explicitly not on revelation but on the basis of natural law. To my knowledge no better framework has been proposed. The American bishops, in a 'reflection' adopted in the autumn of 1993 entitled *The Harvest of Justice is Sown* in Peace, gave a useful summary of Just War thinking and their version is followed here.

1. Just Cause: Force may be used only to correct a grave, public evil, i.e. aggression or massive violation of the basic rights of whole populations.

If we go back to the roots of Just War doctrine we find Aquinas saying (*Summa Theologiae 2a2ae. 40,1*): 'a just cause is required namely that those who are attacked deserve it for some wrong they have done. So Augustine: "We usually describe a just war as one that avenges wrongs, that is, when a nation or state has to be punished either for refusing to make amends for outrages done by its subjects, or to restore what it has seized injuriously. Those wars are looked on as peacemaking which are waged neither from aggrandisement nor cruelty but with the object of securing peace, of repressing the evil and supporting the good"'.

Augustine was thinking primarily in terms of war to resist aggression; one can hear the distant echo of Vandals hammering on the gates of Hippo. But his definition fits modern circumstances. If wickedness is being committed – people killed, populations uprooted – the use of force can be justified to restore what has been seized injuriously. The moral case seems indisputable. Moreover there is considerable support for Augustine's view in contemporary international law.

There is general agreement that, by virtue of its personal and territorial supremacy, a State can treat its own nationals according to discretion. But there is a substantial body of opinion and practice in support of the view that there are limits to that discretion; when a state renders itself guilty of cruelties against and persecution of its nationals in such a way as to deny their fundamental rights and to shock the conscience of mankind, intervention in the interests of humanity is legally permissible.

(L. Oppenheim in **International Law**, Vol 1, Longman, 1948, p. 279)

In a judgement in the House of Lords last March (on the Pinochet case) Lord Millet gave as his view that the doctrine of state immunity is the product of classical theory; that it is a cliché of modern international law that the classical theory in its unadulterated form no longer prevails. Indeed, the way in which a state treats its citizens has now become, for the international community, a legitimate concern. (See *The Times* 29 March 1999). In a remarkably prescient lecture given in 1998 the Secretary-General of the UN, Kofi Annan said that the UN charter protects the sovereignty of peoples; it was not meant as a licence for governments to trample on human rights and dignity. He said that an 'internal' conflict does not give parties any right to disregard basic rules of human conduct, and that all our professions of regret, expressions of determination not to permit another Bosnia or Rwanda, all our claims that we have learned from the recent past would be cruelly mocked if we now let Kosovo become yet another killing field. (See *IHT* 27-28 June 1998). And of course they did.

The British government, commenting on this issue early in 1999, contented itself with observing: 'There may also be cases of overwhelming humanitarian necessity where, in the light of all the circumstances, a limited use of force is justifiable as the only way to avert a humanitarian catastrophe'. (FCO Memorandum to the Select Committee for Foreign Affairs, 22 January 1999). Authorities differ on this point. There can be little doubt however of the moral justification. Where a country is inflicting gross, flagrant and continuing abuses of human rights on its own people, other countries in a position to do so have a right to intervene. Some would say they have a duty to do so (see UNA Policy Statement 2001, Para 3.7) – though Augustine does not go so far. But in other respects he goes further. While some punitive element may well be necessary his emphasis on peacemaking (*pacis studio*) and supporting the good (*boni subleventur*) opens up much wider perspectives. In practical terms these motives can cash out into the form of specific political objectives, such as

- stopping the fighting or enforcing a cease-fire
- preventing the forcible movement of populations, as in 'ethnic cleansing'
- enforcing the delivery of humanitarian aid and safe extraction of the sick and wounded
- restoring pre-existing boundaries or enforcing those newly agreed
- setting up democratic institutions, or most ambitiously
- establishing an international protectorate under UN control

All of these 'causes' and no doubt many others could properly qualify as 'just' under Augustine's rubric.

2. *Legitimate authority: Only duly constituted public authorities may use deadly force or wage war.*
By this Aquinas meant that it is only the sovereign who has the right to go to war, not barons or private warlords. Augustine goes further when (as quoted by Aquinas) he says, 'The natural order conducive to human peace demands that the power to counsel and declare war

belongs to those who hold the supreme authority'. Arguably, if one is intervening for the sake of international peace and good order, then only an international authority has the right to 'counsel and declare war'. This could be a regional organisation such as the Organisation for Security and Cooperation in Europe (OSCE), a Treaty-bound alliance such as NATO or the EU, or even an *ad hoc* coalition as in the Gulf War. But all of these come ultimately under the jurisdiction of the United Nations, both in principle and as a matter of practical politics. It is clear that the United Nations is the supreme source of legitimacy where action in support of international peace and security is concerned, and it is emerging in that capacity in the case of internal conflicts. No one would dispute, indeed the British government explicitly recognised (in the FCO memorandum quoted above) that interventions would preferably be based on an authorisation given by the Security Council under Chapter VII of the UN Charter. The Allied campaign in the Gulf in 1991 and the air campaign against Serbia in 1995 which led to the Dayton settlement had indeed been authorised in this way. But is such endorsement indispensable? Did, for example, the absence of such authorisation in March 1999 render NATO's operation in Serbia and Kosovo illegitimate?

The following considerations are relevant. First, NATO's actions were in no sense arbitrary or ill-considered but the product of unanimous agreement among nineteen democratic nations. Secondly, NATO's actions responded directly to the flagrant disregard by Milosevic of UNSCR 1199 (passed the previous autumn) calling on all parties to cease hostilities. Thirdly, the Security Council had made a singularly ill-judged move at the end of February 1999 by failing to renew the mandate of the UN Preventive Deployment Force (UNPreDep) in Macedonia. This force, some 1,000 strong, had been in place since 1995 and had been much praised as a trail-blazing and successful exercise in pre-emptive deployment. China vetoed its continuance for no better reason than Macedonia's unexpected decision to establish diplomatic relations with Taiwan – an issue totally unrelated to the Balkans crisis. (The Force has never gone back. How very useful it would have been recently). This arbitrary act on the part of China put in question her motives for not endorsing forceful action against Serbia. Sensitivity to her own human rights record might well be relevant, as might the issue of Chechnya in the case of Russia. However, on 26 March, two days after the bombing had begun, a resolution in the Security Council sponsored by Russia, calling on an immediate cessation of violence, was defeated by twelve votes to three – only China, India and Namibia voting in favour. The representative of Slovenia made the robust point that, in his view, the Security Council has the 'primary but not exclusive' responsibility for maintaining international peace and security. This is arguably an accurate reflection of what Article 24 of the UN charter says. Finally the Security Council, by UNSCR 1224 of 10 June 1999, indisputably conferred *post facto* recognition of what had been done, endorsing the 'Petersberg principles' (which I will explain in a moment) and authorising NATO to establish an 'international security presence' in Kosovo.

This episode raises a deeper question. It is clearly too much to hope that the power of veto in the Security Council will never be used for self-serving reasons. Does it then make sense to rest such a veto, on matters relating to humanitarian intervention, in the hands of countries such as Russia or China whose human rights record is so deeply flawed? In my opinion endorsement by the Security Council is a sufficient but not always a necessary condition of legitimate intervention. A more pragmatic argument concerns the effect of NATO's action upon those who choose to see it as unilateral and high-handed. Might this not encourage other parties to act *ultra vires*? The Russians in Chechnya have arguably taken a leaf out of NATO's book, though in fact the circumstances are quite different. It has even been suggested that third parties, fearing similar NATO domineering, might conclude that their best safeguard would be to acquire weapons of mass destruction. This argument is highly speculative, however.

3. Right Intention: Force may be used only in a truly just cause and only for that purpose.

At first sight this looks like tautology: a simple restatement of the Just Cause criterion. In fact it goes much further. Augustine says (again as quoted by Aquinas): 'The craving to hurt people, the cruel thirst for revenge, the unappeased and unrelenting spirit, savageness of fighting on, the lust to dominate and suchlike – all these are rightly condemned in wars'. This should warn us against several misleading motives. It should lead us to be wary of the surge of righteous anger when a city like Dubrovnik is shelled just because it is old and beautiful – and within range of guns: when a family is burned alive for belonging to the wrong religion. It should lead us to be cautious in applying Augustine's earlier remarks about avenging wrongs and punishing. The Allies in the Gulf War set as their aim to evict Iraqi forces from Kuwait, acting under a Security Council Resolution (678 of 29 November 1990) which authorised the use of 'all necessary means' in securing withdrawal of Iraqi forces to positions held before the invasion and the restoration of 'international peace and security in the area.' They did not aim to break the power of the Republican Guards, still less topple Saddam Hussein. When they had succeeded in their limited aim they stopped, the 'savageness of fighting on' was eschewed. Many have since argued that this was a mistake. The Security Council Resolution would arguably have allowed further allied action preventing the use of Iraqi tanks and armed helicopters to suppress the Kurdish and Shia uprisings (which the Allies had incited) and secured Saddam's removal while still stopping well short of Baghdad. This might indeed have achieved a better outcome, but the point can never be proved.

It is a difficult question to what extent self-interest is a necessary ingredient in Right Intention. If not, then how are politicians in a democracy to justify sending young men and women to suffer and (possibly) die where no national interest is involved? How likely is it that, as the price of success mounts, the political constituency, nurtured on television, will lose patience and enforce a humiliating withdrawal, leaving things worse than if force had never been used? Somalia was a vivid object lesson. It is a common criticism of western motives in the Gulf War that the price of oil was the underlying stake, but there was nothing ignoble in that. Poor countries suffer much more than rich ones from high commodity prices – indeed high oil prices can be of direct benefit to producer countries like ours. In Kosovo humanitarian concern for the sufferings of the Albanian inhabitants was clearly the main motive but the 'credibility' of NATO was also at issue. This is seen by some people as American hegemonism and resented accordingly. A more balanced view might be that NATO represents American commitment to European peace and security – which still seems to be indispensable. If so, the credibility of NATO is a good thing and we should support it. Another consideration was that if Milosevic was allowed to have his way in Kosovo it could have led to a wider Balkan war; or at least the encouragement of other villains in other places, from which NATO nations themselves would be bound in the end to suffer. This used to be a popular way of thinking known as 'domino theory', but it is now largely discredited. Or one can contend, following Donne, that no man is an island. Henry Kissinger wrote in IHT, 16 December 1992, that humanitarian intervention asserts that moral and humane concerns are so much part of American life that not only 'treasure' but lives too must be risked in order to vindicate them. He said that in their absence, American life would have lost some of its meaning. He added that no other nation had ever put forward such a proposition, but there I think he was wrong. George Robertson, when British defence minister, insisted that he wanted the British military to be a 'force for good'. So do we all. The problem is that this argument proves too much. If Kosovo, why not Tajikistan or Nagorno Karabakh (both members of the Euro-Atlantic Partnership Council): why not Sudan or Sri Lanka (both of historic concern to Britain) or any other of the twenty-two countries where there are conflicts going on at the moment? Will it do to say that these countries are not on our doorstep or, more to the point, on our television screens? Joseph Nye may have come closer to the mark in saying that another source of enormous disorder would be a foreign policy of armed multilateral intervention to right all such wrongs (see *IHT*, 16 December 1992). It would be going too far to say that self-interest is a necessary ingredient but in my view it is not an illegitimate one – if you will forgive the double negative.

4. *Probability of success: Arms must not be used in a futile cause or in a case where disproportionate measures are required to achieve success.*

Leaving on one side the question of proportion, since this rates as a separate criterion in its own right, this clause introduces a crucial point: that the practicability of what is proposed is a key element in formulating the ethical judgement. It is not a moral act to set the military off on a given course if they are likely to fail, however just the cause. To say this is not to set pragmatism over against morality but to recognise an essential ingredient in the moral judgement itself. If what is proposed will not work then, however lofty the motive, the proposal must be rejected.

One cannot, of course, claim that military forecasts of the likely outcome are necessarily infallible, quite the reverse. The military are often wrong, even on strictly military matters; how else can one account for the fact that, in all the wars of history, roughly 50 per cent of the generals have been losers? One is saying only that they must be asked and their answers heeded.

In Kosovo the initial aim of Operation *Allied Force* was to force Milosevic to accept the substance of the Rambouillet proposals. It was widely expected that a few days bombing would suffice. Failing this, the military aim was starkly defined by General Wesley Clark: 'We are going to systematically and progressively attack, disrupt, degrade, devastate and ultimately destroy these (Yugoslav) forces and their facilities and support. This is not an attack on the Serb people'. (NATO Press Briefing, 25 March 1995)

These aims turned out to have no immediate prospect of success. So far from moving towards the Rambouillet proposals, Milosevic proceeded to vandalise and/or expel the majority of Kosovan Albanians. So far from crumbling in a few days, he stuck it out for seventy-eight. So far from being devastated, the Yugoslav forces in Kosovo survived largely intact. Certainly their freedom of manoeuvre on the ground was seriously curtailed. And NATO quickly achieved air supremacy, at least in the sense of being able to operate without pilot casualties above 5,000 m. But the stated objectives were not attainable and something new was urgently needed. The answer was found in the principles adopted by foreign ministers of the G-8 (i.e. including Russia) on 6 May 1999, often referred to as the Petersberg principles. These required

- Immediate and verifiable end of violence and repression in Kosovo
- Withdrawal from Kosovo of military, police and paramilitary forces

- Deployment in Kosovo of effective international civil and security presences, endorsed and adopted by the United Nations
- Establishment of an interim administration for Kosovo
- The safe and free return of all refugees and displaced persons and unimpeded access to Kosovo by humanitarian aid organizations
- A political process towards the establishment of an interim political framework agreement providing for a substantial self-government for Kosovo, taking full account of the principles of sovereignty and territorial integrity of the Federal Republic of Yugoslavia, and the demilitarisation of the KLA.

These aims proved eminently attainable. Milosevic accepted on 3 June. On 10 June the Security Council underwrote the measures, bombing ceased and withdrawal of Yugoslav forces began, being completed in good order by 20 June. By September the KLA had been effectively disarmed and were being reorganised into the Kosovo Protection Corps; a UN civil presence had been installed and the Albanian population had returned (reportedly some seven hundred and twenty thousand of them) much faster than had been expected or indeed desired. Many intractable problems remained. But as an exercise in ethical pragmatism at a very difficult juncture, the Petersberg principles rate highly. They met in full the criterion of reasonable prospect of 'success' on their own terms. Success in any larger sense is, I agree, much more problematical.

5. Last resort: Force may be used only after all peaceful alternatives have been seriously tried and exhausted.
In other words, if measures short of armed force would suffice then armed force should not be used. Articles 33 to 42 of the UN Charter describe a wide spectrum of measures available to the international community, starting

with enquiry, mediation, conciliation and so forth, via diplomatic and economic measures up to demonstrations, blockade and 'other operations' by land, sea and air forces. Before the Gulf War both Houses of Congress authorised the President to use US armed forces only after he had certified that all appropriate diplomatic and other peaceful means had failed. In many cases it may be appropriate to use these various measures in chronological sequence, only moving up the ladder as and when softer approaches have been tried and failed. But in other instances it may be that to go in early and hard, albeit on a limited scale, might avert much bloodshed. For example, it is widely argued that had the UN, led by the United States, committed ground troops with air support in former Yugoslavia at a much earlier stage (e.g. to prevent the destruction of Vukovar by the Serbs in 1992) it could have nipped that war in the bud. This line of thinking implies a judgement at the outset that gentler methods are bound to fail and that recourse to the methods of last resort (albeit under the general rubric of minimum force) were better taken earlier than later. It is also relevant that economic sanctions, especially when sustained over a long period, can cause just as much suffering to the poorest and weakest in society as a war. The term 'last resort' need not, on this reading, be understood chronologically. In Kosovo, perhaps NATO's action would have been better taken in the autumn of 1998, when it was first authorised in principle. Milosevic's token agreement with terms brought by Ambassador Holbrooke sufficed to let him off the hook.

The two last criteria will be considered together.

6. Proportionality: The overall destruction expected from the use of force must be outweighed by the good to be achieved.
This is the crucial consideration that in effect subsumes all others. It is also arguably the most difficult because it involves weighing in the balance things that, even in

theory, are incommensurable. How many Dutch lives was it worth to protect Srebriniça? Can one put a price on a principle? Yes, one does it every day so there is no dodging, and certainly there are no easy answers. One of the most notable features of recent years has been the way in which the issue of proportionality has dominated at least the vocabulary of debate. Only very rarely have disproportionate interventions been explicitly threatened: for example by the Americans against Serbian Bosnians in summer 1995 and against Saddam Hussein a year later. After the event it is always claimed that the actions have been proportionate.

7. *Noncombatant immunity: Civilians may not be the object of direct attack, and military personnel must take due care to avoid and minimise indirect harm to civilians.*

It is again notable the way in which everyone pays at least lip-service to this consideration. More to the point is the way in which it was taken with all seriousness by the Allies in the Gulf War and by NATO in bombing Bosnia.

In Kosovo it was a crucial feature of Operation *Allied Force* that not only were military targets struck but, as Wesley Clark had promised, their facilities and support. According to the International Institute of Strategic Studies, all oil refining capacity in Serbia was shut down, 50 per cent of military fuel stocks were destroyed and 25 per cent of all fuel stocks. Fourteen power stations were knocked out and sixty-three bridges destroyed as well as many important industrial sites (*Strategic Comments*, Vol 5 Issue 7, September 1999). Michael Binyon, (in *The Times*, on 22 May 1999) accurately prefigured the end of Milosevic's resistance by writing that day after day the vital foundations of daily life were being blown away; he said that blackouts, fuel shortages, blank television screens, broken bridges and regular interruptions to water, gas and sewage systems were leaving a population increasingly bewildered, and that the slow build up had only served to make it worse. An independent group of Serb economists has estimated that 44 per cent of industrial production was destroyed leaving Serbia the poorest country in Europe. (*The Guardian*, 15 October 1999).

Two questions remain. First, could NATO have brought Milosevic to accept the Petersberg principles without attacking Serbia's infrastructure (oil, water, power, telecommunications). Secondly, could the attacks have been more discriminate?

The answer to the first question is almost certainly no. The pressures on Milosevic can be listed as follows, in growing order of importance as one goes down

1. Terms on offer more favourable to Serbia than those at Rambouillet. (They explicitly recognised the involvement of the UN on the ground, involved no automatic referendum on the future of Kosovo and gave NATO no running rights over Serbia other than in Kosovo.)
2. Growing strength of the KLA and effectiveness in forcing Serbs into the open, thus creating targets for B-52s with cluster bombs. (Mount Pastrik 7 June)
3. Disaffection in the Serb military and reluctance of young soldiers to continue
4. Success of NATO attacks on infrastructure (as above)
5. Withdrawal of Russian support prior to G-8 summit at Petersberg, 6 May 1999
6. Milosevic's indictment as a war criminal, which seems to have thrown him off balance
7. The serious prospect (however politically fraught) of a NATO land offensive.

Whilst the ordering of this list is certainly open to question, it seems clear that the last four, at least, were of predominant importance. In the opinion of this writer the attack on infrastructure was a necessary, though certainly not sufficient, condition of 'success'. It is plausible to argue that more emphasis on this aspect, at an earlier stage, might well have brought the bombing to an end sooner and with less loss of life.

NATO apologists maintain, following General Wesley Clark, that Operation *Allied Force* was not a war against the people. The fact remains, however, that leaving aside genuinely accidental damage (and this was serious enough), targets were struck which went beyond any reasonable definition of military. In my opinion such impermissible targets included: a tobacco factory (Nis), food processing plant (Valjevo), bulldozer factory and heating plant (Krusevac), fertilizer factory and petrochemical plant (Pancevo), Zavasta motor plant (Kragujevac), interior ministry, socialist party HQ with TV tower and state TV and radio building (Belgrade). Against this it will be said that some of these, at least, were believed to be dual-use; e.g., car factories were also used to make armoured vehicles. The media facilities were used for war propaganda and incitement to racial hatred. The most inexcusable targets were the Danube Bridges at Novi Sad, far to the north of the country, whose use can have had little impact on operations but whose demolition is continuing to cause huge loss and inconvenience to all riparian states. (Normally 10 million tons a year of grain, coal and ores are carried).

It will be said that every target was approved, at least in principle, by all the participating countries; but doubtless great pressure was brought to bear (for example, by General Wesley Clark on the French) to agree to dubious cases. It is claimed, probably correctly, that a number of targets were owned or controlled by Milosevic's 'cronies'. Dragan Tomic, speaker of the Federal Parliament, was director of Yugo Petrol. Milan Beko, minister for privatisation, was director of the Zavasta plant. Milosevic's son

Marko had extensive tobacco interests. (*IHT*, 20 April 1999). General Short, the NATO air commander, made no secret of his ambition to go hard after Belgrade and the leadership targets and everything that Milosevic 'held dear', and to make it very clear to him that that was exactly what they were doing (*IHT*, 16-17 October 1999). But this objective pushes beyond the limits of proportion and discrimination. Finally, it is claimed that all target dossiers were submitted to legal scrutiny; in which case one has to ask, who was paying the lawyers' fees?

In short, the strongest case against NATO's actions, in the light of Just War criteria, lies in the area of proportion and discrimination. Three further points bear on this issue. First, the fact of bombing (in most cases) from 5,000 metres made discrimination much more difficult and doubtless led to some of the much-publicised cases of admitted accidental damage. The aim was laudable – to save the lives of NATO's pilots and so incidentally prevent the erosion of political support. Many people, not least airmen, have argued that the price in needless damage to civilians was too high. Secondly, the use of precision-guided munitions, particularly against fixed targets whose location and use was precisely known, was a great bonus for proportion and discrimination. It can be argued that *only* precision weapons should be used against such targets in the future. Thirdly, the use of cluster bombs seems morally dubious. NATO officials say that about one thousand one hundred cluster bombs were dropped, containing more than two hundred thousand bomblets, with a failure rate of 5 per cent. It follows that ten thousand or more unexploded cluster bomblets remained. The post war casualty rate in Kosovo (one hundred and seventy up to mid-July 1999) was reportedly comparable to Afghanistan and worse than Mozambique. Nearly half of these were due to cluster bomblets, the remainder being due to anti-personnel mines (*IHT*, 20 July 1999). These figures suggest that cluster bombs deserve to join anti-personnel mines in the category of inhumane weapons.

I launched into the discussion of Just War principles as a means of defending my thesis that war can, in certain circumstances, be the lesser of two (or more) evils. In choosing Kosovo as the worked example I was deliberately going for a very difficult and controversial case. Let me quote one or two more recent examples where I believe military intervention was, or could have been, more obviously beneficial. In the recent report (see www.un.org/peace/srebrenica.pdf) by Secretary-General Kofi Annan on Srebreniça he says

> We (the UN) tried to create – or imagine – an environment in which the tenets of peacekeeping – agreement between the parties, deployment by consent and impartiality – could be upheld ... [But] an arms embargo with humanitarian aid and the deployment of a peacekeeping force ... were poor substitutes for more decisive and forceful action. ...The cardinal lesson ... is that a deliberate and systematic attempt to terrorise, expel or murder an entire people must be met decisively with all necessary means. ... In Bosnia and in Kosovo the international community tried to reach a negotiated settlement with an unscrupulous regime. In both instances it required the use of force to bring a halt to the planned and systematic killing and expulsion of civilians.

And referring particularly to Africa, Mr Annan said in a recent speech (see www.un.org/news/ossg/sgsm_rwanda.htm): 'We have in the past prepared for peacekeeping operations with a best-case scenario. The parties sign an agreement, we assume they will honour it, so we send in lightly armed forces to help them'. 'The time has come for us to base our planning on worst-case scenarios; to be surprised by co-operation if we get it. And to go in prepared for all eventualities, including full combat if we don't … If we don't want to do it properly, should we do it at all? That is what the Security Council members must now ask themselves'.

It is important to recognise how awful many of the postcolonial rebel movements in Africa are. 'Burned down villages, chopped off tongues, mutilated bodies, amputated limbs, raped women and kidnapped children' have been the norm according to Thandika Mkandawire, Director of the UN Research Institute for Social Development. He says 'these guerrilla movements are not exploiting national grievances, and may have no social base at all at the local level. They usually have, literally speaking, nothing to offer' (*Forum*, International Committee of the Red Cross, February 2000, p.34). Sierra Leone is a case in point. The Revolutionary United Front (RUF), however idealistic its origins, soon embarked on the naked pursuit of power and diamonds. Its methods have been unspeakable. The United Nations force, UNAMSIL, had been ineffective to the point of embarrassment. The British Parachute Regiment, in Freetown ostensibly to evacuate civilians, did an excellent strong-arm job in May 1999. It was then replaced by a smaller lightly equipped mission – one-third to train local Sierra Leonean army recruits, the rest to act as protection force. A British patrol, on liaison duty, was captured and humiliated by a gang of thugs. Their rescue was very skilful, but not cost-free. This led to a review of the size, make-up and rules of engagement of the protection force, and an amphibious group arrived to back it up. It is a high-risk operation in a volatile country. But that is not to say we are wrong to be there.

Because, if we choose *not* to go, then we must heed the story of General Romeo Dallaire, Canadian commander of United Nations forces in Rwanda in 1994, the one man who consistently warned of coming slaughter, and sought authorisation to prevent it. He was not allowed to and was so broken by his experiences that four years later he could neither eat, sleep nor concentrate enough to read a newspaper. 'I am in a valley at sunset, waist deep in bodies, covered in blood. I am holding up my arms trying to get out. Each time it comes back the scene is worse. I can hear the rustle of bodies and I am afraid to move for fear of hurting someone'. (Romeo Dallaire, *Shake Hands with the Devil: the Failure of Humanity in Rwanda*, Random House of Canada, October 2003)

These are his post-traumatic nightmares. What had happened was this. In January 1994, he sent a fax to UN headquarters reporting that a Hutu militia informer had told him that they were training men who could kill 'up to 1,000 Tutsi in 20 minutes' and that all Tutsi in the capital were being registered, probably for extermination. General Dallaire's cable was not taken seriously and no action was taken. After the killing began in April he asked for more men and a mandate that would let him intervene. Instead the UN cut his troops. An enquiry five years later agreed with General Dallaire that a few thousand men might have saved 800,000 lives. 'We didn't need overwhelming force, but punctual and appropriate use of force,' he said, 'I needed three battalions in the first three weeks to break the embryo of genocide'. As it was he could do nothing.

So, if one sees a situation in which a state, or an armed faction within a state, is inflicting upon its own people, gross, flagrant and continuing infringements of their human rights (genocide even); if one has the wherewithal in the shape of armed forces with rifles, tanks and guns and the necessary training and skills to stop them; if one chooses to stand aside and let the killing continue then one cannot be surprised if nightmares follow. There is a famous Latin tag from Tacitus: '*Solitudinem faciunt, pacem apellant*' – 'they make a desert and call it peace'. We now know how to promote a better kind of peace. But it *may* take guns to do it.

Summing up

Your question was 'Is war successful in achieving its objectives'. Since the answer to that question is often, and quite obviously 'no' I sought your leave to re-phrase the question as 'Can war be successful in achieving its objectives'. I have argued that in certain circumstances it can be, at least in the sense of being the lesser of evils. What those circumstances are I tried to illuminate by reference to Christian Just War principles. I chose as principal example the case of Kosovo and then looked briefly at some other contemporary instances. I want to say one more thing. Even if military intervention is sometimes the best thing we can do, it can never do more than a very little. In all cases prevention is better than war. This brings in the whole issue of peaceful conflict resolution. Scilla Elworthy talked about this and I will not repeat what she said. Such action is *always* preferable to the use of armed force. But sometimes, sadly, it fails or has not even been tried. We must have ways of coping when this happens. But even when the use of armed force results in the cessation of violence – that is peace as *Pax* the simple absence of war – then begins the far longer and more arduous process of rebuilding the shattered social fabric: peace as *shalom*. The military can play a part in this – unarmed and using their skills as interlocutors, reconcilers, guardians and physical repairers of the infrastructure. But the task is essentially non-military because it involves restoring the economy, political system, rule of law, and civil society. It costs time, money and patience. But it can be done.

So the military can have a part to play in achieving a better peace. But it is a rough and ready tool, a blunt instrument if you like. Its use should always be the last resort. It must be applied with as much precision as possible, and that may not be much. Its role is always the minor one, though it always attracts much publicity. There is no glory in it though there may be death. I have always mentally compared the soldiers' job with that of keeping the drains flowing freely. A dirty job, but someone has to do it.

ISLAM AND THE ETHICS OF WAR AND PEACE (abridged)

Imam Dr Abdul Jalil Sajid

Lecture delivered on Saturday, 18 May, 2002

The evil attacks on the United States on 11 September 2001, apparently by a religiously inspired people, brought worldwide discussion on Islam, the question of Jihad and war, and led a few misinformed and misguided individuals to confuse the Islamic concept of Jihad (struggle against oppression, temptation, evil, and to bring peace and justice) with the medieval concept of 'holy war'. The equation of the two is erroneous and misleading. Holy wars were fought in Medieval Europe in the name of God against infidels, because the latter were perceived to stand against God. Jihad, on the other hand, is fought to repel aggression and lift the oppression of a brutal force, and is never directed at the other's faith. The fact that both are based on religious motivation does not make them equal. I, therefore, do hope that this paper will contribute to a more meaningful discussion of the notion of Jihad, the conception of war (Qital) and peace (Salam) in Islamic tradition. I also hope to be able to illustrate that Islamic world-view and values stand at the side of world peace and global justice, and against aggression and brutality.

Islam and Muslims

Let me begin from the very outset to clarify Islam from Muslim. Most people treat Islam and Muslims as synonymous and mutually interchangeable terms, often saying Islam where they ought to say Muslims and vice versa. In my opinion, the word 'Islam' should be used exclusively for the 'Divine way of Life' based upon its divine sources: The Book known as the Qur'an, 'the word of God' and Sunnah, 'the proven practices of the Prophet' (peace and blessing of God be upon him). 'Muslims' as human beings are free to abide or deviate from divine guidance, as they feel fit according to their own conscience. Islam never claimed to be a new faith. It is the same faith, which God ordained with the creation of the first man sent to Earth. Islam confirms almost all biblical and Hebrew prophets as the Prophets of Islam and their messages as the messages of Islam as long it is confirmed in the Qur'an the Book of Islam. The moral and ethical code of Islam is similar to Judaism and Christianity. The only difference is in theology, concepts and practices in method of worship of the One and the Only One God and methodology, how the morality and ethics should govern all spheres and aspects of our human life.

The main sources of Shariah (Islamic law) are the Qur'an (The Book – word of God) and the Sunnah (the proven practices of the Prophet of Islam), the two chief sources of Islamic jurisprudence. Ijtihad in fact is a rational elaboration of laws either based on the sources or stipulated through human reasoning and self-exertion. Ijma (Ijtihad jamai) or Qias (Ijtihad faradi) etc. are all inter-related, not only under the main heading of Ijtihad but also with the interpretation of the Qur'an and Sunnah.

Political Theory of Islam: Din, Dunya and Dawla

The general theory of an Islamic state begins with a consideration of application of Islamic Shariah in daily life. According to Islamic teachings, the Creator not only laid down laws governing the natural universe but rules for human conduct in all aspects of life. Unlike natural order, which follows its predetermined laws, humankind has the freedom to rebel and follow its own 'man-made' laws, which is, however, a form of unbelief (shirk). Non-submission to the will of Allah is not only an act of ingratitude (kufr) for divine mercies, but also a choice for evil and misery in this world and punishment in the life hereafter. In Islam, all aspects of natural life have been God-willed, therefore, the ultimate purpose of all creation are the compliance of the created with the will of the creator.

Islamic way of life can be summarised in three words 1) Din (religion), 2) Dunya (Community), 3) Dawla (State). Islamic Shariah covers all of these three aspects. From the Islamic point of view, life is a unity. It cannot be divided into watertight compartments. Islamic Shariah gives directions to all aspects of life in its entirety. Islamic Shariah is a complete scheme of life and an all-embracing social order where nothing is superfluous and nothing lacking. Therefore there is no separation between state and church. Secularism, in Muslims' view, destroys the transcendence of all moral values. In Qur'anic words 'those who forget God eventually forget themselves' (59:19) and their individual and corporate personalities disintegrate.

Muslims are required to observe religious rules in the community and establish Islamic state to achieve man's righteousness. It is the duty of every Muslim to cooperate with others for seeking common good. It is the duty of the Islamic state to establish a just social order based on principles of harmony, respect, freedom and dignity where all human beings are accepted with all of their differences.

Diversity is not only recognised but also appreciated in Islamic society. Muslims can discharge this responsibility collectively with establishing an Islamic state with power to command (amr) and prohibit (nahy). Thus Islamic state is an indispensable condition of Islamic life in the true sense of the word 'Islam'.

Sanctity of life

One of the distinctive features of the present world is the overwhelming presence of violence in our societies. The nature of indiscriminate and senseless violence is considered one of the prime threats to the world peace and security. I must make it clear that Islam upholds sanctity of human life, as the Qur'an declares that killing one innocent human being is like killing the entire human race (Qur'an 5:32, 6:151, 17:33), like all other faith traditions. Islam considers all life forms as sacred. The first and foremost basic right of a human being given by God is the right to live in peace and security. However, taking a criminal's life by the state in order to administer justice is allowed in Islam as it upholds the rule of law, and helps maintains peace and security of the society. Only a proper and competent court can decide whether an individual has forfeited his right to life by disregarding the right to life and peace of other human beings. The accused must be given full facilities under the law 'the right of defence'. Extra judicial killings are strictly prohibited in Islam.

Suicide killing

So what about suicide bombing; is this approved in Islam? Suicide bombing and killing one's own self is undoubtedly forbidden in Islam (Qu'ran 4:29), as it is an abuse of the divine gift of life. According to Islamic Law those who commit or try to commit suicide are committing a major sin and will be sent to the fire of hell. Even patients who are in severe pain are prohibited to wish death. The Holy Prophet said: 'Do not harm yourself or injure others'; 'Do not wish death even on the death bed' (Bukhari & Muslim).

The Qur'an says clearly: 'You shall spend in the cause of God; do not throw yourselves with your own hands into destruction. You shall be charitable; God loves the charitable'. (Qur'an 2:195). 'O you who believe do not consume each other's properties illicitly – only mutually acceptable transactions are permitted. You shall not kill yourselves. God is Merciful towards you'. (Qur'an: 4:29) 'Anyone who commits these transgressions, maliciously and deliberately, we will condemn him to Hell. This is easy for God to do'. (Qur'an 4:30) Suicide is a state of disbelief and loss of faith that is condemned by God in the Qur'an. God commands the believers never to despair or lose hope and instead work for a brighter future. '... None despairs of God's grace except the disbelieving people.' (Qur'an 12:87)

The warning in the Qur'an even extends to the surprise that will face those who in despair of God's mercy commit these acts: 'The day will come when each soul will find all the good works it had done brought forth. As for the evil works, they will wish that they were far, far removed. God alerts you that you shall reverence Him alone'. (Qur'an 3:30). 'God advocates justice, charity, and regarding the relatives. And He forbids evil, vice, and transgression. He enlightens you, that you may take heed.' (Qur'an 16:90)

'O people, we created you from the same male and female, and rendered you distinct peoples and tribes, that you may recognise one another. The best among you in the sight of God is the most righteous.'(Qur'an 49:13)

The Qur'an does not call on young volunteers to strap explosives to their bodies and set them off in crowded public areas. The Qur'an does not promise heaven (paradise) as these suicide bombers were taught, but rather warns of condemnation to hell. No promises of paradise or of virgin wives for those suicide bombers can be found in the Qur'an. That much is clear. Suicide bombers are waging a distinctly modern type of warfare not sanctioned in any faith. Many Muslim clerics and scholars have criticised the theology of suicide bombers, and the practice is very controversial within Islam.

Islam's call for peace

Islam is a religion of peace. This fact is borne by both Islamic teachings and the very name of 'Islam'. The term Islam essentially means to submit and surrender one's will to a higher truth and a transcendental law, so that one can lead a meaningful life informed by the divine purpose of creation, and where the dignity and freedom of all human beings can be equally protected. Islamic teachings assert the basic freedom and equality of all peoples. Islam stresses the importance of mutual help and respect, and directs Muslims to extend friendship and good will to all, regardless of their religious, ethnic, gender, cultural, linguistic or racial background.

Islam, in fact, makes peace at every greeting, which Muslims exchange whenever they meet by saying, 'Peace be unto you' (Assalamu 'Alaykum). The Muslim also utters this statement at the end of every ritual prayer. From its inception, the Qur'an emphasised peace as an intrinsic Islamic value. In fact, the terms 'Islam' and 'Peace' have the same root, 'salaam'. Furthermore, God has chosen the word 'peace' (salaam) as the Muslim's greeting to remind believers as one of God attributes.

Islam, on the other hand, permits its followers to resort to armed struggle (Qital) to repel aggression, and indeed urges them to fight oppression, and injustice. But for some, Jihad or Qital is nothing more or less than a 'holy war', i.e. a war to enforce one's religious beliefs on others. Most Muslims would reject the equation of Jihad with holy war. There are still small and vocal groups of Muslims who conceive Jihad as a divine licence to use violence to impose their will on anyone they could brand as an infidel, including fellow Muslims who may not fit their self-proclaimed categorisation of right and wrong.

Peace in Islam does not mean the absence of war, but the absence of oppression, corruption, injustice and tyranny. Islam considers that real peace can only be attained when justice prevails. Islam therefore justifies war against regimes that prevent people from choosing their ideals and practicing their beliefs. It does not, however, justify war against non-Muslim entities. The Islamic society should thus maintain peace with those who show good will to Muslims. In international law, there is a set of well-established rules concerning the obligations of nations towards each other in times of war and peace. The first of these is that a country should base its relations with other countries on terms of peace so that it may exchange benefit and cooperate with others in order to promote humanity to utmost perfection. Peaceful ties like these, they say, should not be broken except in extreme urgencies that necessitate war, provided that all peaceful steps have failed in terminating the cause of dispute.

This is what Islam has always been working for, and the relations of Muslims with others are primarily based on peace. Muslims refuse to fight merely because others do not embrace a faith, nor does Islam allow Muslims to fight against those who disagree with them on any religious basis. Islam urges its followers to treat such people kindly: 'God does not enjoin you from befriending those who do not fight you because of religion, and do not evict you from your homes. You may befriend them and be equitable towards them. God loves those who are just and equitable.' (Qur'an: 60:8).

In another place, God says: '... Therefore, if they leave you alone, refrain from fighting you, and offer you peace, then God gives you no excuse in fighting them'. (Qur'an 4:90). Muslims are told, 'If they resort to peace, so shall you, and put your trust in God' (Qur'an 8:61). Instructions like these pave the way for the establishment of peace, and helps to set down principles that call for the abolishment of war.

Reviewing the early Muslim era and reflecting on the experience of the early Muslim generations, one can clearly see that peace was always the original position of Muslims, and that war was either a punitive measure to annihilate tyranny and oppression, or a defensive measure to stop aggression. From the very beginning, Prophet Muhammad was instructed to use a friendly and polite approach to call people to Islam. 'Invite to the way of your Lord with wisdom and beautiful preaching; and argue with them in ways that are best and most gracious.' (Qur'an 16:125)

Despite the violent opposition of the Quraysh, the Prophet proceeded to summon people peacefully to Islam, and the Muslims were further commanded, for prudential reasons, not to respond to the violence of the Quraysh. Muslim pacifism during the Makkan period was a political tool to influence change and to protect Muslims from mass destruction. After the immigration to Madinah, the Muslims were permitted to fight against those who declared war against them.

The Prophet Muhammad, peace and blessings be upon him, was the peacemaker of his time. He endured torture, hunger and the killing of his loved ones by his enemies, but he remained a merciful person. In his bloodless conquest of Makkah he forgave his archenemies. In his twenty-three years of struggle for Islam, the total number of people who lost their lives from all sides was less than seven hundred in wars that were imposed upon him. Islam is a religion of peace and tolerance. There is an abundance of Quranic and historical evidence to show that it does not approve of coercion. Throughout the thirteen years of his mission in Makkah, the Prophet disallowed the use of force by his followers even though non-believers persecuted them.

Jihad in Islam

Jihad is one of the most misunderstood of Islamic terms used today, and many Muslims are as confused by it as non-Muslims. Few words carry as much power to instil fear or hatred. That's because the news media have widely interpreted Jihad to mean 'holy war', linking it with extremism and terrorism in the public consciousness.

The concept of Jihad has nothing to do with aggressive warfare or 'holy war'. The word 'Jihad' finds its origin in the verb 'jahada', which means to struggle with one's utmost effort to remain Muslim and to exert oneself to establish peace and justice. The word 'Jihad' has a few different connotations, since struggle can occur on several levels. Muslims understand these levels based not only on the words of Allah in the Qur'an, but also on the authentic statements of the Prophet Muhammad as recorded in our oral traditions, preserved as 'ahadith'. Jihad refers to any effort, mental, moral or physical, made to make God's word supreme. It covers a wide range of activities, from fighting inside oneself against one's own evil promptings, to being engaged in war for the cause of Islam. Here are the levels of Jihad:

- *Personal Jihad*: Prophet Muhammad Ibn 'Abdullah (may the peace and blessings of Allah be upon him) said, 'The most excellent Jihad is that of the soul.' This Jihad, called the Jihadun-Nafs, is the intimate struggle to purify the soul of satanic influence – both subtle and overt. It is the struggle to cleanse one's spirit of sin. This is the most important level of Jihad because one fights against one's own temptations, ignorance and weakness.

- *Verbal Jihad*: On another occasion, the Prophet said, 'The most excellent Jihad is the speaking of truth in the face of a tyrant.' He encouraged raising one's voice in the name of Allah on behalf of justice.
- *Physical Jihad*: This is combat waged in defence of Muslims against oppression and transgression by the enemies of Allah, Islam and Muslims. Muslims are commanded by God to lead peaceful lives and not transgress against anyone, but also to defend ourselves against oppression by 'fighting against those who fight against us'. This Jihad 'with the hand' is the aspect of Jihad that has been so profoundly misunderstood in today's world.

Qital fi sabil-Allah (fighting for sake of Allah)

Qital (fighting and waging war), a word often used in the Qur'an, is the highest form of Jihad. It is not an act of aggression for the sake of material interests or a wanton display of national or tribal power, but it is a sacred duty assigned to every Muslim in the interests of humanity so that there should be peace and justice in the world. The word 'Jihad' is often confused with the word 'Qital' (fighting) and these are used in one and the same sense, whereas the Qur'an has made a clear distinction between Qital and Jihad fi Sabil Allah (fighting for the sake of God). The Qur'an has also clearly pointed out that Jihad denotes two kinds of strivings; striving with the help of God-given faculties, both mental and physical, and striving with the help of resources which one has at one's command.

The Qur'an on war, peace and justice

The aim of war according to the Qur'an is not to propagate or spread Islam, nor is it to expand the territory of the Islamic state or dominate, politically or militarily, non-Muslim regions. Rather, the aim of war is to establish and assure justice, and to annihilate oppression and abolish tyranny. It is true that the right to communicate the message of Islam is protected under Islamic law, and the Islamic society must, therefore, respect and defend this right. But the obligation to protect the right of Muslims, and for this matter all religious communities, to promote their belief and values should be carried out through peaceful means and in a friendly manner. The assurance of justice and destruction of tyranny are therefore the underlying objectives of war. However, since the terms 'justice' and 'tyranny' cover wide ground and permit broad interpretation, they need to be translated into more concrete forms. We can distinguish five situations where the violation of the principle of justice and the excessive misconduct of tyranny call the Islamic society to war and justify its use of violence against the political entity that is implicated in such practices.

1. War against oppression

It is incumbent upon Muslims to challenge any political authority that either uses its free exchange of ideas, or prevents people from freely professing or practicing the religion they chose to embrace.

> And fight them until there is no more persecution and religion is only for Allah ... (Qur'an 2:193)

> And why should ye not fight in the cause of Allah and of those who, being weak, are oppressed – men, women, and

children, whose cry is: 'Our Lord, rescue us from this town, whose people are oppressors; and raise for us from Thee one who will protect; and raise for us from Thee one who will help.' (Qur'an 4:75)

It should be made clear here that oppressiveness of a particular regime is not to be determined by comparing the values and conduct of that regime with Islamic norms and standards, but rather by its toleration of the Muslim interaction with its subjects and the communication of Islam to the general public. Corruption and mismanagement should not be considered, therefore, the criteria that classify a particular regime as oppressive, deserving, thus, to be fought, because, it may be recalled, Muslims are commanded to invite humankind to Islam through friendly and peaceful means and effect social and political change using the peaceful methods of education and moral reformation. Only when their peaceful efforts are frustrated and met with violence, are they justified to use violence to subdue the aggressive party. As it was shown above, the Prophet did not resort to war against the pagan Arabs until they persecuted the Muslims and violated their lives and properties. Similarly, the Prophet declared war against Byzantium and its Arab allies only when they killed the messengers and missionaries who were sent to peacefully summon people to Islam and introduce to them the new revelation of God.

2: War in defence of Muslims

When wrong is inflicted on a Muslim individual by a member, or members, of another community, whether this wrong is done to his person, by assaulting or murdering him, or to his property by robbing or unjustly confiscating it, the Islamic state is obligated to make sure the individual, or his family, is compensated for his suffering, and that his rights are upheld. Because it is beyond the scope of this paper to discuss the legal procedure of this matter, it suffices to say that the Islamic state should ensure that justice has been done to the wronged Muslim, even if that takes a declaration of war against the political community that tolerates such an aggression, provided that the authority of the political community has refused to amend the wrong inflicted on the Muslim individual after it has been formally notified and given reasonable time to respond. ' ... Whoever then acts aggressively against you, inflict injury on him according to the injury he has inflicted on you and be careful (of your duty) to Allah and know that Allah is with those who guard (against evil)'. (Qur'an 2:194).

Upon examining closely the Qur'anic passages in which God permitted Muslims to fight, we find that they clarify that war should be a means to drive away aggression and tyranny

> Permission is granted to those who are being persecuted, since injustice has befallen them, and God is certainly able to support them. They were evicted from their homes unjustly, for no reason other than saying 'our Lord is God.' If it were not for God's supporting of some people against others, monasteries, churches, synagogues, and mosques – where the name of God is commemorated frequently – would have been destroyed. As for victorious Believers, God says, 'They are those who, if we appointed them as rulers on earth, they would establish the system of obligatory regular prayers (Salah) and the obligatory charity (Zakat), and would advocate righteousness and forbid evil, God is the ultimate authority' (Qur'an, 22:39-41).

Military victory should not lead to expansion or dominance as the case is with colonial regimes, nor should it lead to control over sources of wealth, or to arrogance in the land to raise a race above another. Victorious believers had better 'establish regular prayers' to attain spiritual exaltation by worshipping God, and to purify their spirits. They 'establish the obligatory charity' and thus establish social justice by supporting the right of the needy to live a decent life. They 'advocate righteousness 'by spreading benevolence and right among people, and ' forbid evil' by fighting against evil and corruption and uprooting them from society. The Prophet fought only to drive away aggression, after having received his divine orders: 'You may fight in the cause of God against those who attack you, but do not accede the limit as God does not like aggressors' (Qur'an 2:190).

3. War against foreign aggression

The clear-cut case of foreign aggression is a military attack on the Islamic state or its allies. The Muslims, however, are not obliged to wait until the enemies launch their attack, to respond. Rather, the Islamic state can initiate war and carry out a pre-emptive strike if the Muslim authorities become convinced beyond a shadow of a doubt that the enemy is mobilising its forces and is about to carry out an offensive, or if a state of war already exists between the Islamic state and its adversaries.

If aggression is committed against another political entity with which the Islamic state has entered into mut-ual alliance, or has signed a treaty that stipulates protection, the Islamic state is also obliged to fulfil its commitment to its ally and provide the military support needed. The conquest of Makkah was precipitated by Quraysh's attack on Khuza'ah, which was an ally of the Islamic city-state of Madinah, thereby violating a provision of the Treaty of al Hudaybiyah that prohibited such an act. Polytheists used different methods to inflict harm on Muslims. Finally they decided to kill the Prophet. When the latter learned of the intention, he emigrated to Medina and was warmly welcomed by its people who pledged allegiance to him in the cause of Islam. The atheists were not content with trying to kill the Prophet, but also provoked non-Muslim tribes against him in order to put an end to his message. When the case reached this stage, God gave permission to Muhammad to fight.

4. Fighting for the cause of Justice and Truth

The Muslims are commanded to establish justice and peace on earth. This requires Muslims to stand in the face of injustice and oppression, wherever they may be, and eradicate their causes, and not to take hold of the Earth, or enslave people or dominate their welfare, but establish the word of God on Earth, without doubtful intentions. In Islam, this is called the 'strife in the cause of God' and the 'Fight in the cause of God' (Qur'an 2:244 and 22:78). The cause of God is the cause of justice. Every fight in the cause and support of freedom in religion is a fight in the cause of God; and every fight to drive away oppression and support the oppressed against the oppressor, or to support right and justice is a fight in the cause of God. Every effort done to attain or protect justice is also done in the cause of God.

The Qur'an demands believers to fight in the cause of God, without any worldly intentions. The following verses, sent down to the Prophet in Medina, clarify the aims of war

> Those who readily fight in the case of God are those who forsake this world in favour of the hereafter. Whoever fights in the cause of God, then gets killed, or attains

victory, we shall surely grant him a great recompense. Why should you not fight in the cause of God when weak men, women, and children are imploring: 'Our Lord, protect and save us from this community whose people are oppressive, and be You our Lord and Master'. (Qur'an: 4:74-75).

A hint is made here that, in Islam, war is not for oppressing or enslaving people; it is waged for the cause of God and weak people, like those in Makkah who were persecuted and oppressed by the Makkan atheists. It is the duty of every believer to support people like these and relieve them from oppression, people who no longer have any supporter and thus turn to God for refuge.

Those who believe are fighting for the cause of God, while those who disbelieve are fighting for the cause of tyranny. Therefore, you shall fight the devil's allies; the devil's power is nil. (Qur'an 4:76)

Evil means transgression of limits. Thus when one transgresses limits and behaves arrogantly in the land, enslaves others and deprives them of their rights or of having a share in the riches of the earth, he is said to be fighting 'in the cause of Evil' which God criticises severely and considers as the motto of atheists. The aim of fighting in the cause of God is to spread divine law (which calls for justice and freedom of religion) in the world without there being any selfish intent or arrogance in the land, as God wants the case to be: 'We reserve the abode of hereafter for those who do not seek exaltation on earth, nor corruption. The ultimate victory belongs to righteous' (Qur'an: 28:83).

To this effect, Muhammad sent his delegates to eight neighbouring rulers with messages calling them to embrace Islam. The appeal was rejected. Some of them even killed the Prophet's delegates, and some tore the message and threatened the delegates who had brought it. The rulers of the time were a clear obstacle in front of the individuals' freedom and their right to live in justice and to choose their religion freely. Islam was the civilised step in the development of humankind. Islam declared war against an obsolete form of tyrannical governing. If Islam used force, then it was only to enforce justice that resulted in fascinating civilisations in every area where Islam entered.

5. War of law enforcement

When a proportion of the population residing within the boundaries of the Islamic state breaks the rule of law, or threaten the territorial integrity of the Islamic state, the Muslim authorities are justified in using armed force to subdue the rebellion. It should be emphasised, however, that what is at issue here is not just opposition to a particular public policy, but an insurrection that attempts to achieve its goals through military tactics, threatening thereby the lives and property of other members of the society. Three types of dissension, however, should be differentiated, two of which are merely causes of rebellion, which can be forcefully subdued, while the third is a case of legitimate political opposition that should be dealt with in a peaceful manner.

Global Ethics and Interfaith Dialogue

I am reminded the words of Professor Hans Kung 'No peace among nations without peace among the religions and no peace among the religions without dialogue between the religions' (at World Parliament of Religions, Chicago 1993: 'Towards Global Ethics'). I add: 'No peace without Justice and no Justice without forgiveness and compassion'. Dialogue and agreement must be conscientiously applied and maintained, so to create bonds of love, care, trust and confidence. Its prerequisite is proper education and learning from one another. We must speak and act truthfully with compassion. We must treat others as we wish others to treat us. Every human being must be treated fairly, humanly and with dignity without any fear or discrimination.

I admire the work of Prince Hassan El Talal over the years for promoting better understanding between different faiths and advocating dialogue for resolving conflicts. His short book *Continuity, Innovation and Change* is a must-read for every Muslim (First published July 2001 by Majlis El Hassan, The Royal Court, Amman, Jordan). I not only share his vision but also say that he represents true Islamic scholarship in the current debate on the issue of world peace. The building of peace requires an attitude of sanctity and reverence of life, freedom and justice, the eradication of poverty, dissolution of all forms of discrimination and the protection of the environment for personal and future generations.

Conclusion

This is a brief sketch of those rights, which fifteen hundred years ago Islam gave to humankind, to those who were at war with each other. The world has not been able to produce more just and more equitable laws of Islam than were given fifteen hundred years ago. On the other hand it hurts one's feelings that Muslims are in possession of such a splendid and comprehensive system of ethics of war and peace and yet they look for guidance to those leaders who could not have dreamed of attaining those heights of truth and justice. Even more painful than this is the realisation that throughout the world the rulers who claim to be Muslims have made disobedience to their God and the

Prophet as the basis and foundation of their own government. May God have mercy on them and give them the true guidance. May God guide us all and show us the right path of true and everlasting peace in this world in our lifetime. Amen.

Selected Bibliography

Abu Sulayman, Abdul Hamid, The Islamic Theory of International Relations: Directions for Islamic Methodology and Thought (Herndon, VA: The International Institute of Islamic Thought), 1408 AH/1987 AC

al Ghunaimi, Mohammad Talaat, *The Muslim Conception of International Law and the Western Approach* (Netherlands: Martinus Nijhoff/The Hague), 1398 AH/1978 AC

Arnold, T.W., *The Preaching of Islam* (London: Constable and Company), 1332 AH/1913 AC

Hamidullah, Muhammad, *Muslim Conduct of State*, 7th ed. (Lahore: Muhammad Ashraf, 1961)

Haykal, Muhammad H., *The life of Muhammad*, translated by Isma'il al Faruqi, 8th ed. (North American Trust Publications), 1396 AH/1976 AC

Ibn Rushd, 'Chapter on Jihad', in *Bidayah al Mujtahid wa Nihayah al Muqtasid*, translated by Rudolph Peters in *Jihad in Mediaeval and Modern Islam* (Belgium: E.J. Brill), 1397 AH/1977 AC

Johnson, James Turner, and John Kelsay (eds.), *Cross, Crescent, and Sword: The Justification and Limitation of War in Western and Islamic Tradition* (New York: Greenwood Press, 1990)

Johnson, James Turner, and John Kelsay (eds.), *Just War and Jihad: Historical and Theoretical Perspectives on War and Peace in Western and Islamic Tradition* (New York: Greenwood Press, 1991)

Khadduri, Majid, *War and Peace in the Law of Islam* (New York: AMS Press), 1399 AH/1979 AC and *The Islamic Law of Nations: Shaybani's Siyar* (Baltimore, Maryland: The Johns Hopkins Press), 1386 AH/1966 AC.

Kolocotronis Jamila, *Islamic Jihad: An Historical Perspective* (American Trust Publications, 1990)

Mawdudi, Abul *Ala, Al-Jihad fil Islam* (Urdu) Darul Musanifeen Azam Gragh (UP-India) 1930

Peters, Rudolph, *Islam and Colonialism: The Doctrine of Jihad in Modern History* (The Hague: Mouton, 1979) and *Jihad in Classical and Modern Islam* (Princeton: Markus Wiener, 1996)

Reuven Firestone, *Jihad: The Origin of Holy War in Islam* (Oxford University Press, 1999)

THE HUMAN COSTS OF WAR

Dr Paul Grossrieder

Lecture delivered on Saturday, 13 July 2002

Sickness is felt, health little or not at all. – Montaigne

Though we often focus on the technical aspects of wars, such as how they are fought, who conducts them, and what causes them to break out, it is rare that consideration is given to the core of the problem of war. It is rare that armed conflict is presented in terms of its tragic effects on individuals and communities. Perhaps the reason for this is to be found in the very culture of war, which was long considered a matter for professionals. Indeed, until the Second World War, it was true that war concerned principally, if not only, combatants and other military personnel. Accordingly, war was viewed as a series of heroic acts that had only minor effects on civilians. From Homer's Achilles to the towering generals of the First World War, the great virtues of the victors, as humans and as warriors, were celebrated. The sufferings of the people, including women, the elderly and children, were viewed as slight and unintended. In addition, far fewer people were affected then than today. The wars of religion were of course horrific, and marked by unspeakable massacres, but in those wars too the victors were untroubled by such tragedies, since they fought in the name of divine justice and truth.

From the wars of independence to today's international terrorism, the situation has changed. Civilian populations have frequently become the focus of conflicts: combatants take them hostage, and the civilian victims no longer suffer only as a result of the fighting between armies, but are themselves directly targeted. Since 1945, 84 per cent of the people killed in wars have been civilians, and the average annual number of deaths has been over half a million.

I shall therefore limit my comments to current conflicts, describe and analyse the many kinds of problems they cause in human terms. The concrete inhumanity of the wars will appear. What would anthropologists arriving from another planet and noting the human cost of today's wars have to say? How can any sense be made of the 24 million people displaced within their own countries, or of the 18 million forced to flee to foreign lands? The displacement and emigration are a direct result of the conflicts. They undermine all efforts undertaken to improve people's lives within their own countries.

According to a survey carried out by the ICRC in a dozen countries (People on War) more and more wars are being fought against civilians, especially unarmed civilians. In Colombia, Angola, the Balkans, and eastern Congo for example, people have regularly been terrorised by groups of combatants. Displaced people, acting heads of households, and children separated from their parents are among the victims of this terror. More and more people go 'missing', while women are bought and sold. Some refugees and displaced people have been able to return home after long periods of conflict, as in Cambodia, Mozambique or El Salvador. But others, such as all Palestinian refugees since 1948, retain this 'status' for a very long time – indeed, for far too long. Over a million Afghans are living in Pakistan because of a war that began in 1979.

Women and children, the first victims in today's wars

Security is a major problem for women and children, who are especially likely to be forced to leave their homes and left to their own devices, without anyone to protect them from ill-treatment of all kinds. Conflicts destroy society's very foundations and engender a subculture of violence where conduct without regard for any rule becomes the norm.

Women are subject to *sexual violence*, which can be a form of torture, a means of obtaining information or a punishment for acts actually or supposedly committed. Sexual violence can also be used to destroy ethnic identity, or even as a means of war: 'Rape and sexual violence [have] been used to assert dominance over your enemy. Since women's sexuality is seen as being under the protection of the men of the community, its defilement is an act of domination asserting power over the males of the other community or group that is under attack.'(Radhika Coomaraswarmy, *A question of honour: Women, ethnicity and armed conflict*, International Centre of Ethnic Studies, Third Minority Rights Lecture, Geneva, 25 May 1999, p. 4)

Women who have been raped suffer both physical and social repercussions. If, for cultural reasons or under duress, they have no other choice but to have their child, they may be ill-treated in their community or completely ostracised. They may be accused of prostitution, adultery or bringing dishonour upon their families. Children who are born in these circumstances are also often excluded from society.

At the time of the massive *displacements* from Kosovo to Albania, UNHCR noted that there was trafficking in women for the sex trade. This is one of the problems that can result from population movements in conflict situations. In some cases, civilians have been forced to leave their homes and property by parties threatening them with attack as part of an ethnic-cleansing campaign, or using them as human shields.

The UN Office for the Coordination of Humanitarian Affairs estimates that 80 per cent of displaced people are women and children, which suggests that they are the most vulnerable people and the first to be threatened by combatants. Sometimes, as was the case in the former Yugoslavia, men are prevented from fleeing for ethnic policy reasons. In camps, it is difficult for women to carry out their traditional roles of preparing meals and caring for the sick. On a regular basis, their lives are severely disrupted. Women's showers, for example, may be located too near those of the men, which deprives them of privacy as they wash. In camps in Tanzania, UNHCR attempted to offer single women better protection by providing them with orange tents; in reality, this put them in greater danger, as the tents made them easier to locate.

Civilians' *freedom of movement* is also impeded in times of conflict owing to mines, military roadblocks and snipers, the immediate result of which is that it becomes difficult to obtain food, water and traditional herbs. Once again, women are especially exposed to danger as they are expected to perform tasks traditionally falling to men, such as cultivating fields, conducting business, and feeding livestock.

Access to *food and water* is sometimes restricted for military reasons. Heads of households (women or older children) should, however, be able to move about to perform basic tasks for the sake of the family's survival. Sanctions imposed by the UN Security Council 'to maintain or restore international peace and security' (Charter of the United Nations, Art. 39) are also among the obstacles to these tasks being accomplished. Since the end of the Second World War, the UN has imposed more and more economic sanctions (such as those against South Africa, the former Yugoslavia, Haiti, Iraq, Rwanda and Sudan).

The risk of famine resulting from the sanctions should be taken into consideration by the Security Council before any application of Article 41 of the Charter.

When people are displaced, they find themselves without the kitchen utensils and stoves needed to prepare food. They may also lack water, for example because their camp is located outside the area supplied or because the water available is barely adequate to cover the needs of the resident population. A lack of water affects the displaced people's hygiene and consequently their health, as they may suffer from such ailments as diarrhoea, typhus, cholera, hepatitis A, etc.

Conflicts also result in women and children taking charge of *agricultural production*. In view of the traditional division of labour between men and women, this represents a considerable change of role for women. Even positive social changes such as this one are sometimes accompanied by tensions, however. After the genocide in Rwanda, for example, great concern arose about the absence of property rights for widows, who were thus at risk of being evicted from their farms or prevented from returning to them. During fifteen years of war in Sri Lanka, according to the Marga Institute, wheat production decreased by 27 per cent, onion and potato production by 64 per cent and the quantity of fish caught by 63 per cent.

Displaced civilians are generally forced to *abandon their livestock* and other goods. When this happens, they must seek another livelihood. In the Congo, in 1994, it was the women who started small commercial activities, such as sales of bread and fish. The aim of course was to regain a measure of economic independence.

Life in camps for displaced persons involves *health* problems, in particular communicable diseases such as HIV/AIDS among women who have had to engage in sexual relations in exchange for food. Displacements within infected areas contribute to renewed outbreaks of malaria.

Civilians can be injured in connection with fighting and yet not admitted to hospitals, which are primarily reserved for combatants. Mine injuries and amputations cause severe psychological trauma.

In human terms, the worst consequences of war are connected with the break-up of the *family* and the collapse of the *educational system*. Family members are often separated and without news of each other. At the end of a conflict, some will be declared 'missing'. Although it is families that are directly affected, whole societies are deeply shattered and relations among groups that were enemies during the conflict are further damaged. 'Suppressing grief can lead to an inability to deal with other traumas of armed conflict, to lack of healing and to prolongation of the conflict and of hostilities and divisions within communities; it can even lead to an unwillingness for reconciliation between different sides.' (*Women Facing War*, ICRC, Geneva, 2001, p. 132)

The lack of teaching in schools during wars has disastrous consequences on society as a whole, and especially on young people. In Angola, for example, the school system in the countryside has been practically non-existent for some thirty years. The only training of any kind that has persisted concerns the male population only and consists merely of combat training. Girls are left to their own devices and are illiterate.

The sufferings of host communities

Despite their suffering, those driven from their homes are outnumbered by other victims of war. The communities that play host to them, whether within or outside their own country, are often extremely poor – which does not prevent them from being very hospitable. At the end of 1996, thousands of people from Kivu offered what little they had to those who were fleeing from eastern Zaire.

Throughout the 1990s war in Liberia, those who fled the fighting were supported by poor rural communities just as much as by international aid.

In 1994, almost all jobs for unqualified workers in the town of Goma were taken by refugees who had just arrived there. With help from aid organisations, they were able to accept salaries that were only one half or even one third of the – already low – salaries of resident workers.

Communities that play host to displaced people and refugees may well be the group that is most forgotten.

Children who kill

Children are not always innocent victims. In Rwanda, more than forty children have been accused of genocide. According to the Machel Report, two hundred thousand children across the world were involved, often voluntarily, in no fewer than twenty-four conflicts in the 1990s.

In Sierra Leone in 1995, the Revolutionary United Front went from one village to another, recruiting children and forced them to be present at, or even to take part in, the execution of their families. They were then drugged and taken to neighbouring villages to continue killing. ('Sierra Leone out of the bush', *The Economist*, 6 May 1995)

Psycho-social suffering

The psycho-social suffering caused by war has only recently been widely recognised. In Mozambique, 44 per cent of women have witnessed a murder, 25 per cent have been separated from their children and 30 per cent have been tortured. (J. El Bushra and E. Piza Lopez, *The Development in Conflict: The Gender Dimension*, Oxford Discussion Paper No 3, 1993/1994, p. 63). Men, women and children who have experienced war suffer among other things from the deep personal wounds resulting from the loss of family members or friends, and of personal objects and sources of income, the impact of which generally cannot be measured in strict economic terms. For such people, life can lose all meaning, and beliefs and ideals can be called into question. They have witnessed or have had to take part in atrocities, or have themselves been subjected to torture or rape. The survivors may feel guilty that they have survived or suffer from not having done more to prevent acts of violence against others. All this can cause unbearable trauma. By way of illustration, let us quote the account of a Sarajevo resident: 'I am afraid,' he said. 'I can no longer go through a tunnel or cross a bridge. In the tram, I am sometimes dizzy, and I feel like I want to kill myself or the other passengers. I am constantly haunted by visions of fighting. My mind is unstable and unwell. My life is ruined.' ('Après-Guerre(s)', Collection Mutations, No. 199/200, January 2001, p. 21)

Hostage populations

Thus far, I have considered only the 'direct' human cost, so to speak, of war, i.e. the harm caused by today's conflicts to civilian individuals and groups. But an even more tragic situation arises when parties to the conflict, for the sake of economic advantage or military victory, take entire civilian populations hostage for long periods of time. In Angola, for example, the government and the armed opposition both condemned innocent civilians to famine. Now, hordes of barefooted people are coming out of the bush who are totally destitute and famished. Editorial in *Le Monde*, 18 May 2002, said that in Angola both the government and Unita waged a ruthless war, carrying out a scorched-earth policy. This involved taking civilian populations hostage. Tens of thousands, if not hundreds of thousands, of skeleton-like, dazed people were waiting for aid to arrive. This is the result in human terms of the so-called 'humanitarian blockade' imposed on the population under the control of the rebel movement.

This description illustrates the degree to which armed conflicts leave their mark on societies, by breaking them up, destroying family unity and leaving hopeless, failed communities.

The human consequences of armed movements' business interests

The end of the Cold War brought about a spectacular decrease in outside support for local wars. As a result, the warring parties in internal conflicts launched business ventures so as to obtain the wherewithal to pursue their war efforts. Were it not for their business interests, the Khmer rouge, for example, could not have survived after Chinese support ended. With accomplices in Thailand, they began to traffic in precious stones, wood, and antiques.

All these activities are illegal. Moreover, the control of resource-rich territories – not the relative well-being of the people living there – is the chief tactical aim of these groups. At the same time, the destruction of the enemy's resources can be another primary objective. This change in local conflicts has also led to the formation in developed countries of diasporas actively supporting rebel movements.

One last scenario is the one that causes local people to suffer most. When armed movements have no resources available to them in the territory where they operate, shortages occur. The factions will use any means necessary to ensure their own survival. They will not hesitate to take whatever they need by force, even if doing so jeopardises the local economy that is sustaining them. This kind of activity is one of the causes of famine in Somalia and in southern Sudan. (This analysis is developed by J.M. Balencie, A. De La Grange and J.-C. Rufin in *Mondes rebelles*, Vol. 1, Michalon: Paris, 1996)

What should be done?

In view of the human disaster caused by wars, reason would seem to require that there be a universal movement to compel all humanity to tackle the causes of war, so as to eradicate it once and for all and put an end to the absurdity of its human consequences. Unfortunately, war is not subject to reason, and the force of emotion, beliefs, and ethnic identity is such that war repeatedly disrupts the lives of nations. To attempt to slow the pace and frequency of this chronic recourse to war, and to 'humanise' armed conflicts, remains an all-important duty. How should it be performed?

• The power of images: the images of atrocities in the former Yugoslavia, in Somalia and Rwanda were part of our mental geography in the 1990s. In Bosnia and Somalia (and to a certain extent, and belatedly, in Rwanda), media coverage eventually prompted diplomatic and military action from western governments in the summer of 1995. Other conflicts that have been just as destructive, such as those in Colombia, Liberia and Sudan, have not benefited from the same degree of coverage.

  When the human cost of war is prominently reported, public opinion intensifies its rejection of violence and strongly insists that it be stopped, and that 'something be done'. This puts pressure on governments.

- A need to *protect civilians*: as soon as wars break out, policies should be put in place to protect civilians and prevent the warring parties from targeting them. This amounts to taking the Geneva Conventions seriously. The Conventions remain up-to-date in terms of their content, but suffer from a lack of political will to make sure they are applied. Changing the subject to the alleged obsoleteness of international humanitarian law is pointless. To do so is but a pretext for not applying the rules. The States Parties, if they so desire, are perfectly capable of respecting these rules and ensuring respect for them. Were they to do so, the human cost of war would be sharply reduced.

- A need for *prevention*: if States ever seriously compared the costs of war with those of prevention, they would recommend that their foreign ministries negotiate, in the Security Council for example, preventive deployments of peacekeepers. The cost would be far lower than that of intervening after a conflict has broken out. In Macedonia, for example, prevention peacekeeping troops have cost US$ 8 million. Compared with the US$ 134 million cost of NATO's intervention in Bosnia in 1996, the investment in Macedonia was well worth it.

- The *mobilisation of multinational companies*: companies doing business in countries at war should develop codes of conduct and comply with the principles of international humanitarian law. These companies cannot be satisfied with merely respecting the environment; they must also respect the civilian population and local communities.

Conclusion

By way of conclusion, I shall read a few lines to you from the correspondence of Peter Paul Rubens on the horrors of war and 'fortress Europe' (which is strikingly topical, now as ever). The passage was written in 1638 when the Franco-Spanish war was laying waste to Flanders and Picardy. Like the master's paintbrush, it reveals horror, suffering and despair in the face of violence, destruction, the crushing of civilisation and general ruin.

> The principal figure is Mars, who has left the open temple of Janus (which in time of peace, according to Roman custom, remained closed) and rushes forth with shield and bloodstained sword, threatening the people with great disaster. He pays little heed to Venus, his mistress, who, accompanied by her Amors and Cupids, strives with caresses and embraces to hold him. From the other side, Mars is dragged forward by the Fury Alekto, with a torch in her hand. Nearby are monsters personifying Pestilence and Famine, those inseparable partners of War. On the ground, turning her back, lies a woman with a broken lute, representing Harmony, which is incompatible with the discord of War. There is also a mother with her child in her arms, indicating that fecundity, procreation, and charity are thwarted by War, which corrupts and destroys everything. In addition, one sees an architect thrown on his back with his instruments in his hand, to show that that which in time of peace is constructed for the use and ornamentation of the City, is hurled to the ground by the force of arms and falls to ruin. I believe, if I remember rightly, that you will find on the ground under the feet of Mars a book as well as a drawing on paper, to imply that he treads underfoot all the arts and letters. There ought also to be a bundle of darts or arrows, with the band which held them together undone; these when bound form the symbol of Concord. Beside them is the caduceus and an olive-branch, attribute of Peace; these also are cast aside. That grief-stricken woman clothed in black, with torn veil, robbed of all her jewels and other ornaments, is the unfortunate Europe

who, for so many years now, has suffered plunder, outrage, and misery, which are so injurious to everyone that it is unnecessary to go into detail.

(Letter from Peter Paul Rubens to Justus Sustermans commenting on his painting *The Horrors of War*, 12 March 1638.)

THE ENVIRONMENTAL COSTS OF WAR

Professor Paul Rogers

Lecture delivered on Saturday, 13 July 2002

Compared with the effects on people and on economies, the environmental effects of war have so far been relatively limited. At the same time, they can be severe under certain circumstances, war industries can have serious local impacts and some forms of conflict could potentially have calamitous results. Moreover, there are examples of wars that have already had severe environmental impacts, and these should give us concern for the future.

What is much more significant in relating environmental issues to conflict is the existence of profoundly important relationships between environmental processes and the causes of conflict. In this talk I want to cover both aspects, broadening out the theme to examine environmental interactions and war rather than limit ourselves to environmental consequences of war. I will do this in the belief that human interactions with environmental processes, at both the regional and global levels, are going to be key factors in the evolution of international conflict in the coming decades.

But let us look first at the environmental effects of war.

Environmental effects of war

Most forms of conflict involve violent actions directed specifically at opponents and their economies. In their most extreme form these can involve the wholesale destruction of armed forces in the field, and the targeting of civilian populations in their towns and cities. Such actions inevitably have major environmental side-effects, examples being the utter destruction on the western front in the First World War, the destruction of cities, dams, irrigation systems and many other features.

The side effects on natural environments are severe, but they are usually relatively short-term. In part this is because ecosystems have a remarkable capacity for regeneration, especially when areas of intense destruction are surrounded by relatively unscathed zones. Even the wholesale destruction in Flanders was remedied by a couple of decades of re-growth, and the huge swathes of bomb damage in East London in the 1940s resulted in the colonisation of sites by the ecosystem that was to last for years until the city was rebuilt.

In short, wars up until now have inevitably had their major effects on people and their societies. Even so, there have been important exceptions. Significant among these has been the impact of war industries, especially at times of major conflict. In such circumstances, any semblance of pollution control and other forms of environmental safeguards have been discounted, with massive consequent damage.

Many of the examples of environmental damage in the north of England were particularly significant during the First and Second World Wars. In Huddersfield, for example, there was the wholesale destruction of one of the most beautiful woodlands in the town as a result of air pollution caused by munitions production as local dye-works were subsumed into the war effort in the First World War. This beauty spot, Kilner Bank, was reduced to a deeply acidic wasteland (pH1.5) and was not restored to anything approaching its original state until an innovative land restoration project in the early 1970s.

More recently, we have seen the far more massive side-effects resulting from the development of the nuclear weapons industry. Extensive radioactive contamination resulting from nuclear testing has been a feature of large areas of land in New Mexico and Nevada in the United States, parts of Siberia and the Russia Arctic, and areas of South Australia, French Polynesia and other Pacific islands and, almost certainly, parts of China.

In Britain, the Windscale fire in the 1950s spread contamination across much of Cumbria, there are reliable reports of serious contamination following an accident in a nuclear waste deposit in the Soviet Union at about the same time, and there is a substantial problem of disposal relating to Soviet-era nuclear submarine reactors. The United States nuclear weapons industry has been plagued by problems of waste disposal, with much of it closed down in the early 1990s, in part, because of these problems. Rocky Flats and Hanford River both have clean-up problems running into billions of dollars and the environmental and human costs in Russia are reported to be massive.

Although not directly related to nuclear weapons, the radioactive contamination resulting from the incident at Chernobyl has given us some idea of the effects of a nuclear war, with the nearby city of Pripiat abandoned as being far too costly to decontaminate.

Since the end of the Cold War we have learnt that the much-derided estimates by peace researchers of the likely consequences of a nuclear war were actually remarkably accurate. If Britain had been subject to a 100-megaton attack, up to 40 million of the population of 56 million would have died, and much of the country would have been reduced to a radioactive wasteland.

Moreover, work done towards the end of the Cold War established that a central nuclear exchange between the superpowers would, besides killing hundreds of millions of people in the short-term, have created a two-year nuclear winter which would have devastated the human communities and natural environments of most of the northern hemisphere.

Apart from the possible effects of nuclear war, a risk which is still with us, there are a number of examples of the environmental effects of conflict that indicate the capacity for destruction. One is the pernicious effect of anti-personnel land-mines, removing land from production for generations. There remain large tracts of NW Egypt that are still no-go areas as a result of mines laid at the time of the battle of El Alamein, and more recent use of land-mines involves devices that are more difficult to detect and clear.

A second is the use of area-impact weapons such as napalm, cluster bombs and fuel-air explosives, all of which are intentionally destructive over a wide area. While aimed at people, they also have an environmental impact that can have a lasting effect on surviving communities. Moreover, there have been noted occasions where there has been the intentional destruction of large areas of natural forests and also crops, as a means of restricting insurgents. This was a technique developed by the British in Malaya and taken up on a much larger scale by the United States in its use of the notorious Agent Orange in Vietnam. More recently, the most noted example of deliberate environmental damage was the destruction and firing of the Kuwaiti oil wells by retreating Iraqi forces in 1991.

Even so, the environmental effects of war may be severe, and could be calamitous in the event of nuclear use, but the more significant connection between environmental systems and conflicts lies in a range of interactions that relate partly to resource location and use and partly to the longer-term impact of human effects on the global ecosystem.

These two features represent one of two core drivers of potential conflict in the coming years and should be analysed alongside the other, the rapidly growing disparity between a relatively small global elite of around a billion people and an increasingly educated yet marginalised majority of five billion.

The violent effects of increasing socio-economic polarisation are already apparent, with a likely trend towards further instability and conflict. On its own, this is, at the very least, a matter for real concern. It might therefore be argued that such a trend will be recognised, and that sufficient economic reforms might be put in place to curb an excess of insecurity. There are few signs of this happening and it would, in any case, have little effect unless it was part of a recognition of the second global trend, the growing impact of environmental constraints on human activity.

In essence, the limitations of the global ecosystem now look likely to make it very difficult if not impossible for human well-being to be continually improved by current forms of economic growth. This is certainly not a new prognosis, and formed a central part of the frequently derided 'limits to growth' ideas of the early 1970s. Those ideas stemmed from some of the early experiences of human/environment interaction, notably the problems of pesticide toxicity, land dereliction and air pollution, all initially significant problems in industrialised countries.

The earliest indications came in the 1950s with severe problems of air pollution affecting many industrial cities, most notably a disastrous smog episode in London in 1952, responsible for the deaths of some four thousand bronchitic and elderly people. A decade later came the recognition of the effects of organophosphorus pesticides on wildlife, a process greatly stimulated by a single book, Rachel Carson's *Silent Spring*. Later in the 1960s there were environmental disasters in Europe including a massive fish kill in the Rhine, the wrecking of the *Torrey Canyon* oil tanker near the Scilly Isles and the killing of over one hundred and forty people, mostly children, when a coal mining waste tip engulfed a school in the village of Aberfan in Wales.

By the early 1970s, environmental concern was sufficient to stimulate the first UN Conference on the Human Environment in Stockholm. Although initially likely to be concerned with the environmental problems of industrialised states, the Stockholm meeting was substantially influenced by an early systems study of global environmental trends, *Limits to Growth*, published a few months earlier (Donella H. Meadows, Dennis L. Meadows, Jorgen Randers and William H. Behrens III, *Limits to Growth*, London: Earth Island, 1972).

While widely criticised as a somewhat crude simulation study of the global system, *Limits to Growth* was seminal in introducing the idea that the global ecosystem might not be able to absorb the overall effects of human activity, especially those stemming from the highly resource-consumptive and polluting lifestyles of the richer states of the industrialised north.

The early signs of environmental problems were joined by much more significant changes in the past two decades. Air pollution became recognised as a regional phenomenon through the experience of acid rain, and a global problem, the depletion of the ozone layer, began to be recognised as serious in the 1980s. Ozone depletion has a significance as being the first major global effect of human activity. It resulted from the effects of a range of specific pollutants, chlorflourocarbons (CFCs) and related chemicals, on the thin layer of ozone in the upper atmosphere that normally shields the Earth's surface against excessive amounts of UV radiation.

While the potential for an ozone depletion problem was recognised in the 1970s, concern was hugely boosted by the discovery in the early 1980s of an annual 'ozone hole' over the Antarctic each spring. The problem was brought under some degree of control by international agreements, specifically the Vienna Convention in 1985 and the Montreal Protocol two years later, but still had a large effect on environmental thinking – this was a human activity that was having a discernible and potentially devastating impact on the entire global ecosystem.

Other problems developing on a global scale also rose to prominence. They included desertification and deforestation, the latter having an immediate effect in terms of soil erosion and flooding, and the salinisation of soils, especially in semi-arid areas. Other forms of resource depletion became evident, most notably the decline in the resources of some of the world's richest fishing grounds, not least in the continental shelf fishing grounds of North America and Western Europe.

Problems of water shortages and water quality are already severe in many parts of the world. Around half of the population of Southern Asia and Africa does not have access to safe drinking water, and 80 per cent of diseases in these areas stem from unsafe water.

At a more general level, there have been tensions between states over the status and use of major river systems.

The 1959 agreement between Egypt and Sudan resulted in joint control over the mid-Nile waters, but Ethiopia controls 85 per cent of the sources of the Nile, with Sudan and Egypt having the prime dependencies. Similarly, the Ganges and Brahmaputra rivers are essential to Bangladesh, with its rapidly growing population. Schemes for joint utilisation exist with India and Nepal, but Bangladeshi requirements and Himalayan deforestation remain twin pressures.

A more specific source of potential conflict is the substantial Turkish programme of dams, hydro-electric and irrigation programmes on the upper waters of the Tigris and Euphrates rivers in South East Anatolia, rivers which are subsequently essential to the economic well-being of Syria and Iraq.

Also in the Middle East, a much smaller-scale problem that forms a largely hidden part of Israeli-Palestinian negotiations is found in the West Bank. Winter rainfall on the West Bank hills provides water not just for the West Bank, but also for much of Israel in the form of underground aquifers flowing westwards towards the Mediterranean. Any long-term settlement will require a fair sharing of the water resources that will be very difficult to achieve given the already heavy use of water by Israel and the increasing water demands in both Israel and the West Bank.

In some parts of the world a persistent failure to come to terms with human environmental impacts produced near-catastrophic results. Nowhere was this more clear than in many parts of the former-Soviet Union, with a drying-out of the Aral Sea, massive problems of pesticide pollution and the radioactive contamination of Arctic environments the most obvious examples.

Individual problems of pressures on land, water, fisheries and other resources are likely to increase, notwithstanding some successful cross-border agreements, as population growth and increases in *per capita* resource consumption combine in their effects. Even so, two much more broad global phenomena will have a more profound impact on global security, the 'resource shift' and climate change.

Resource shift

The resource shift is a centuries-old phenomenon that stems from the original industrial revolutions of Europe and North America feeding initially on domestically-available raw materials, whether coal, iron ore, copper, tin, lead and other non-renewable resources. In the early nineteenth century, European industrial growth was based largely on such resources mined within Europe, and the much more resource-rich United States could continue to be largely self-sufficient until the latter half of the twentieth century.

Much of the era of colonial expansion was predicated on requirements for resources, and many of the colonial wars, so costly to the newly-colonised peoples, stemmed from the determination to control land and supplies of raw materials.

In the past century, the industrialised north has become progressively more dependent on physical resources from the south, as its own deposits of key ore, coal, oil and gas have become progressively more costly to extract. This resource shift has meant that certain physical resources have acquired a strategic significance that, in a number of cases, already results in actual or potential conflict.

Zaire, for example, has had much of its politics in the forty years since independence dominated by competition for the control of Shaba Province, formerly Katanga. This has included outright violence during the civil war after independence in 1960, and rebellions in Shaba in 1977 and 1978 that were helped by Eastern Bloc aid from neighbouring Angola and were controlled by Franco-Belgian military interventions with logistic support from NATO.

At the root of these conflicts has been the formidable mineral deposits of Shaba. Of these, the best known may be copper and industrial diamonds, but of at least as great significance are the cobalt mines around Kolwezi and Mutshatsha, these deposits representing about half of known world reserves in the late 1970s. With cobalt a key component of ferro-cobalt alloys used in ballistic missile motors, jet engines and other defence-related products, preventing the control of the Shaba deposits falling into the hands of leftist rebels was a priority.

The protracted and bitter twenty-five-year conflict for the control of Western Sahara between Morocco and the independence-seeking Polisario Front has complex causes, but a central factor is the massive reserves of rock phosphates at Boucraa in the north of the country. Rock phosphates form the basis of phosphate fertilisers, in turn the essential components of compound fertilisers used throughout world agriculture. On its own, Morocco is the world's main exporter of rock phosphate, but with the Western Sahara reserves it achieves near-dominance.

Elsewhere in Africa, illicit trading in diamonds has fuelled conflicts in Sierra Leone and Angola, much of the western support for South Africa during the apartheid years was a consequence of South Africa's dominance of gold and platinum markets, and Russian determination to maintain control of parts of the Caucasus is due, in part, to access to Caspian Basin oil.

Even so, transcending all of these is the geo-strategic significance of the oil reserves of the Persian Gulf region, reserves that are both remarkably plentiful and cheap to extract. At the end of the twentieth century, some two-thirds of all the world's proved reserves of oil were located in Persian Gulf states with production costs typically around $3 a barrel compared with up to $12 a barrel for oil from more difficult fields such as the North Sea or Alaska.

When the Iraqi army occupied Kuwait in August 1990, the Saddam Hussein regime added Kuwait's oil fields to its own even larger deposits, gaining control of 19.5 per cent of all of the world's known oil reserves. Saudi support for the subsequent coalition military build-up stemmed, to a large degree, from a fear that the Iraqis would go on to seek control of the massive Saudi oilfields close to Kuwait. With Saudi oil then representing over a quarter of all known world oil reserves, the western coalition perceived the Iraqi regime as threatening to control 45 per cent of the world's oil, an entirely unacceptable prognosis demanding reversal.

The exploitation of world oil reserves is a remarkable example of the resource shift in that the world's largest consumer of oil, the United States, was until the early 1970s self-sufficient, but is now a massive oil importer. During the 1990s, in particular, the United States progressively ran down its own reserves of easily extracted oil, while new reserves proved elsewhere in the world typically increased the holdings of many countries.

To be specific, the US had reserves totalling 34 billion barrels in 1990; these decreased by more than a third during the decade, whereas the proven reserves of Saudi Arabia, Iraq, Kuwait and the United Arab Emirates, all much larger than those of the US, actually increased. Thus, in all of these states, the discovery of new reserves exceeded production. By the year 2000, all the major industrialised states of the world, except Russia but including China, were becoming progressively more dependent on Persian Gulf oil, even allowing for the deposits of the Caspian Basin.

Overall, and throughout the twentieth century, the industrialised states of the north have become progressively more dependent on the physical resources of the south, a trend set to continue well into the new century. As a potential source of conflict it is a core feature of the global economy.

Climate change

Of the many environmental impacts now being witnessed, one stands out above all the others – the development of the phenomenon of climate change as a result of the release of so-called greenhouse gases, especially carbon dioxide and methane. One of the most fundamental of modern human activities, the combustion of fossil fuels, is demonstrably affecting the global climate. Among the many effects already apparent and likely to accelerate are changes in temperature and rainfall patterns and in the intensity of storms.

The greenhouse effect caused by increases in gases such as carbon dioxide in the atmosphere has been recognised for some decades, and it was initially expected to have its most notable impact in terms of increases in atmospheric temperature – hence the use of the term 'global warming'.

In the past two decades this has become recognised as a pronounced oversimplification of much more complex changes in the world's climate, including considerable regional variations. It has also been more widely recognised that there are substantial natural climatic cycles, some of which, such as the El Nino effect in the Pacific, may also be affected by human activity. Furthermore, other forms of atmospheric pollution resulting from human activity might even counter the effect of the greenhouse gases.

A further complexity is that it has been generally believed that the more pronounced effects of climate change would happen in temperate regions, with tropical latitudes largely buffered against substantial change, a belief based on some historical evidence that the tropics had been least affected by earlier natural climatic cycles. The expectation has been that there would be substantial effects on north and south temperate latitudes and on polar regions. The former might variably involve changes in rainfall distribution, increases in temperature and increased severity of storms.

There would be gainers and losers but the major effects of global climate change would be felt, by and large, by richer countries that would best be able to cope. Some commentators saw it as ironic that those countries that had contributed most to greenhouse gas production would be the countries most affected by climate change.

Not all the effects of climate change would impact on temperate latitudes, and two effects have long been expected to cause substantial problems for poorer countries. One is the likelihood of more severe storms, especially cyclones. While rich industrialised countries may be able to cope, albeit at a cost, the changes affecting poor countries will be well beyond their capabilities to handle.

There are examples of this across the world, and it is sometimes possible to contrast the impact of such disasters on rich and poor countries. In 1992, Hurricane Andrew hit parts of the United States, killing fifty-two people and causing damage estimated at $22 billion, over 70 per cent of it covered by insurance. Six years later, Hurricane Mitch hit Honduras and Nicaragua. The death toll was eleven thousand, and less than 3 per cent of the $7 billion damages were insured.

The other effect is the risk of sea level rises, stemming partly from an expansion of the oceans consequent on increases in temperature and partly from a progressive if slow melting of polar icecaps. Effects of both of these trends would be severe on a number of poorer countries, partly because some of the heaviest concentrations of population are in low-lying river deltas, but more particularly because of the lack of resources to construct adequate sea defences.

Such problems have been recognised for some time, but more recent analysis of climate change, over the past five to ten years, suggests another pattern of effects that are likely to have much more fundamental global consequences. Although predictions are tentative, evidence has accumulated that the anticipated buffering of climate change in tropical regions may not happen, or at least may be far less pronounced.

In particular, there are likely to be substantial changes in rainfall distribution patterns across the tropics, with the overall effect being far less rain falling over land and more falling over the oceans and the polar regions. With the exception of parts of equatorial Africa, almost all the other tropical and sub-tropical regions of the world are likely to experience a 'drying out'.

The impact of this is likely to be fundamental in terms of human well-being and security. Across the world as a whole, the great majority of people live in these regions, most of the countries are poor, and most produce their own food, primarily from staple crops dependent on adequate rainfall or irrigation. Much of the food is still produced by subsistence agriculture. Most of the heavily populated areas are the major river valleys and fertile deltas, including the Nile, Indus, Ganges, Brahmaputra, Mekong and Chanjiang (Yangtze) and areas of high natural rainfall across Latin America, sub-Saharan Africa and South East Asia.

A substantial drying-out across the tropics will have a hugely greater effect than any likely impact on temperate latitudes for two reasons. One is that the basic ecological carrying-capacity of the land – its ability to support given human populations – will decline, and the second is that poor countries will have massive difficulties in trying to adapt their agricultural systems to limit the loss in food production.

Some of the most substantial changes of the last half century have happened with little warning. Perhaps the most serious crisis of the Cold War, over the Cuban missiles in 1962, came virtually out of the blue. The oil price rises of the early 1970s were almost entirely unexpected, the anticipation throughout the west being of an era of cheap and plentiful oil. The Iraqi invasion of Kuwait in 1990 erupted out of nowhere in a matter of weeks.

These are examples of political crises, albeit two of them with resource overtones, but it is also the case that assessing environmental trends, especially at the global level, is frequently difficult – pesticide toxicity in the 1960s, acid rain in the 1970s and the sudden intensity of ozone depletion in the 1980s being among a number of examples.

There has been considerable progress in the study of the global ecosystem in the past half century, especially in terms of the knowledge of the mechanisms of biogeochemical cycles, oceanic systems and the global climate, but all of these are, at the very best, imperfectly understood. As a consequence, there is every possibility that many current expectations concerning human environmental impacts may be incorrect. It is possible that some of the warnings now being made, including those discussed above, may turn out to be excessive as natural control mechanisms come into play and moderate the effects of the impacts.

This might be considered reassuring, but there are several reasons for thinking that such optimism is unwarranted. The first is that many of the expected effects are likely to prove costly and politically unwelcome. As a result where significant environmental research is undertaken in publicly-funded centres, whether government laboratories or universities, there is a tendency for researchers to be cautious in their conclusions. If the implications of your research results are unpalatable, you tend to be very careful in ensuring that you are as certain as you can be with the evidence.

The second is that there is growing evidence from various long-term fossil and other evidence, that the global ecosystem, especially its climate, has been much more volatile than was previously thought. In other words, natural 'buffering' systems may not have coped with induced change in the past. Finally, the time-scales of human interaction are much more immediate in terms of 'ecosystem time' than anything short of rare natural cataclysms such as a massive meteor or comet striking the Earth, one explanation for the extinction of the dinosaurs.

Humans evolved over several million years, but only spread right across the world by twenty thousand years ago, numbering perhaps five million before they learnt to farm ten thousand years ago. Cities and empires have developed in the past five thousand years but environmental impacts were limited in extent and confined to a few locations until the start of the industrial revolution just over two hundred years ago. Only since then have there been major regional impacts and only in the past one hundred years can these be said to have 'gone global', with most of that effect coming in the closing decades of the last century.

In other words, a global ecosystem evolving over several billion years was hardly affected by its most intelligent species until the most recent century, but that one species is engaging in activities that do just that. In such circumstances, it is probably wise to err on the side of caution and expect the unexpected to cause further problems rather than be a solution to them.

Summarising

To summarise the argument so far, the current economic system is not delivering economic justice, and there are now firm indications that it is not environmentally sustainable. This combination of wealth disparities and limits to current forms of economic growth is likely to lead to a crisis of unsatisfied expectations within an increasingly informed global majority of the disempowered.

Such a crisis, as seen from the elites of the north, is a threatening future. As Wolfgang Sachs puts it

> The North now glowers at the South from behind fortress walls. It no longer talks of the South as a cluster of young nations with a bright future, but views it with suspicion as a breeding ground for crises.
>
> At first, developed nations saw the South as a colonial area, then as developing nations. Now they are viewed as

risk-prone zones suffering from epidemics, violence, desertification, over-population and corruption.

The North has unified its vision of these diverse nations
by cramming them into a category called 'risk'. It has
moved from the idea of hegemony for progress to hegemony for stability.

In Sach's view, the north has utilised the resources of the
south for generations but has now come up against environmental limits to growth

Having enjoyed the fruits of development, that same small
portion of the world is now trying to contain the explosion
of demands on the global environment. To manage the
planet has become a matter of security to the North.
(Quoted in Paul Rogers' *Losing Control: Global Security in the
Twenty-first Century*, Pluto Press, 2002)

Managing the planet means, in the final analysis, controlling conflict, and within the framework of the devel-
opment/environment interaction, several issues are
likely to come to the fore, stemming from migratory
pressures, environmental conflict and anti-elite violence.
None of these is new and there are recent examples of
all.

Potential sources of conflict

Potential sources of conflict stem from a greater likelihood
of increased human migration arising from economic,
social and especially environmental desperation. This
movement will focus on regions of relative wealth and is
already leading to shifts in the political spectrum in recipient regions, including the increased prevalence of nationalist attitudes and cultural conflict.

Such tendencies are often most pronounced in the most vulnerable and disempowered populations within the recipient regions, with extremist political leaders and sections of the popular media ready to play on fears of unemployment.

This trend is seen clearly in Western Europe, especially in countries such as France and Austria, where antagonism towards migrants from neighbouring regions such as North Africa and Eastern Europe has increased markedly. It also figures in the defence postures of a number of countries, with several southern European states reconfiguring their armed forces towards a 'threat from the South' across the Mediterranean.

There are already some 30 to 40 million people displaced either across state boundaries or within states, and this figure is expected to rise dramatically as the consequences of global climate change begin to have an effect. The pressures are likely to be particularly intense from Central into North America, Africa and Western Asia into Europe and South East Asia towards Australia. The most probable response will be a 'close the castle gates' approach to security, leading in turn to much suffering and not a little 'militant migration' as marginalised migrants are radicalised.

Perhaps least easy to assess is the manner in which an economically polarised and increasingly constrained global system will result in competitive and violent responses by the disempowered, both within and between states. There are already many examples of such actions, whether the Zapatista revolt in Mexico, or movements stemming from the disempowered in North Africa, the Middle East and Southern and South East Asia.

At an individual and local level, much of the response from the margins takes the form of criminality, usually by young adult males and directed not just against wealthier sectors of society but often against the poor and unprotected. For middle-class elites in many southern states, though, security is an everyday fact of life, with people moving from secure work-places through travel in private cars to gated communities and leisure facilities with twenty-four-hour protection. For the richest sectors of society, security extends to armed bodyguards and stringent anti-kidnapping precautions, with a host of specialist companies offering their services.

This is the environment that is already the norm throughout most countries of the south, and the widening rich/poor gap suggests it will get worse. But the more difficult and potentially more important problem stems from substantial new social movements directed, often with violence, against the elites. Predictions are difficult but four features are relevant.

The first is that anti-elite movements may have recourse to political, religious, nationalist or ethnic justifications, with these frequently being fundamentalist, simplistic and radical. Many recent analyses focus on the belief systems themselves, with much emphasis placed by western writers on religious fundamentalisms, especially within the Islamic world.

While such religious movements are significant, they are far from being alone in serving as a motivation against marginalisation and for empowerment, with ethnic, nationalist and political ideologies, cultures or beliefs also being of great significance. At times, it is as if the 'Islamic threat' is being erected to replace the Soviet threat of the Cold War years, an attractive yet thoroughly dangerous simplification of a much more complex set of processes.

The second feature is that anti-elite movements may be more prevalent in the poorer states and regions of the world, and they may therefore be considered of little concern to the relatively small number of wealthy states that dominate the world economy. But in an era of globalisation, instability in some part of the majority world can have a considerable effect on financial markets throughout the world, making the security of local elites of real concern to the west. Wealthy states are dependent on resources from the south, on cheap labour supplies and on the development of new markets for their advanced industrial products. Fifty years ago, a civil disturbance in a country of the south might have its effect in the north within weeks. Now, it can be within minutes.

Thirdly, there is a perception across much of the majority world that a powerful and firmly rooted western hegemony is now in place and a very widespread response is one of real antagonism to this control of the world economy. It is easy to assume, from a western ethnocentric position, that antagonisms are most likely to be directed from the margins at local elites. This is not necessarily the case. There is, instead, every chance that it is the western economic dominance that will be blamed for marginalisation, not the activities of local elites.

Finally, there is sufficient evidence from economic and environmental trends to indicate that marginalisation of the majority of the world's people is continuing and increasing, and that it is extremely difficult to predict how and when different forms of anti-elite action may develop. It was not predictable that Guzman's teachings in Peru would lead to a movement of the intensity and human impact of Sendero Luminosa, nor was the Zapatista rebellion in Mexico anticipated. When the Algerian armed forces curtailed elections in 1991 for fear that they would bring a rigorous Islamic party to power, few predicted a bloody conflict that would claim many tens of thousands of lives.

What should be expected is that new social movements will develop that are essentially anti-elite in nature and draw their support from people, especially men, on the margins. In different contexts and circumstances they may have the roots in political ideologies, religious beliefs, ethnic, nationalist or cultural identities, or a complex combination of several of these.

They may be focused on individuals or groups but the most common feature is an opposition to existing centres of power. They may be sub-state groups directed at the elites in their own state or foreign interests, or they may hold power in states in the south, and will no doubt be labelled as rogue states as they direct their responses towards the north. What can be said is that, on present trends, anti-elite action will be a core feature of the next thirty years – not so much a clash of civilisations, more an age of insurgencies.

The economic geographer, Edwin Brooks, put it succinctly thirty years ago when he said it was so important to avoid

> a crowded glowering planet of massive inequalities of wealth, buttressed by stark force yet endlessly threatened by desperate people in the global ghettos.
>
> (See *'The Implications of Ecological Limits to Growth in Terms of Expectations and Aspirations in Developed and Less Developed Countries'*, in Vann and Rogers [eds.] Human Ecology and World Development, Plenum Press, 1974)

Conclusion

To avoid such a dystopic world requires immense energy and commitment as we seek the processes of socio-economic and political change that will help us achieve a more just and sustainable world order. The next ten years will be of fundamental importance in achieving this and our work and progress in this direction may well determine the shape of much of the new century.

> This lecture draws, in part, from Chapter 5, "The New Security Paradigm" of *Losing Control: Global Security in the 21st Century*, Paul Rogers, Pluto Press (Second Edition) June 2002

THE UN AND THE FUTURE OF GLOBAL GOVERNANCE

Sir Crispin Tickell

Lecture delivered on 17 May 2003

In a lecture series on *Preparing for Peace*, I hope you will forgive me if I begin with the Iraq war. Not just because it is topical, but because it has clear implications for the United Nations, multilateralism and global governance.

- The war was begun in circumstances which in effect abandoned the multilateral approach to international problems, and in the words of the UN Secretary-General was 'not in conformity with the Charter' (http://www.wagingpeace.org/articles/2004/09/16_un_lessons-iraq-war.htm)
- Its legality was questionable, and has in fact been widely questioned by the vast majority of lawyers. Excuses for it ring increasingly hollow
- Like all wars it will have effects on the global as well as the local environment, and the problems involved in limiting damage to it
- It has also highlighted divisions between the world's industrial countries. Inevitably they take the leadership in global governance.

In short, the war has been bad for the United Nations and bad for multilateralism, and bad for global governance.

Can the United Nations bounce back? Of course it can. The United Nations has proved surprisingly robust over the last fifty years. It has survived extraordinary changes in international relationships, and adapted itself pretty well in the process.

Five main changes

I was the witness of five main changes, or groups of changes during my time as British Permanent Representative between May 1987 and September 1990. First and most obvious were the changes in attitude caused by the ending of the Cold War. The process was astonishingly rapid. Suddenly Permanent Representatives were able to talk to each other with a measure of common understanding and purpose. This was particularly so within the Security Council, and among the Five Permanent Members who found themselves at last able to fulfill most of the role given them under the Charter. New combinations developed among them: on some issues I found myself closer to our former adversaries than our friends. I was the informal chairman of the Five for almost two years. Some of our first essays in the management of crises took place in my apartment looking over the East River.

I was also the witness of the general replacement of confrontation by cooperation among the vast majority of United Nations members. This was despite the north-south polarity created by the break-up of the old colonial empires and a vast increase in its membership. Many of the new members had seen the United Nations less as a guardian of the status quo than as an agent of change to put right inequities between states. The arguments between rich and poor, between so-called developed and so-called developing countries, over such notions as new world economic orders or new world information orders had long proved sterile. Those who sang hymns to development were rarely clear about what they thought development meant. Many of the underlying problems remain unresolved (and indeed have got worse since then). A new approach to them was – and is – clearly required.

At the same time I was the witness of a new willingness to contemplate the use of force in the name of the international community. A real test came in the reaction to the Iraqi invasion of Kuwait, and the creation of the coalition under United Nations auspices to expel the Iraqis. This coalition was a classic example of the United Nations exerting the powers given it under the Charter. There had been a clear invasion of one sovereign state by another. Since then, for example in the Balkans, the United Nations has struggled to define its role in the face of far messier civil wars. But despite all failures and shortcomings, the Security Council remains the only global institution responsible for managing international peace and security.

I was also the witness of the development of new attitudes towards national sovereignty, a political concept first given legal force by the United Nations Charter. So far, respect for sovereignty has been a foundation stone of the United Nations and its various institutions. Those who have the least sovereignty are always keenest to protect it. But over the years recognition of the constraints on it has become general, and erosion of the practice if not of the concept of sovereignty is widespread. Generally states are no longer watertight – if they ever were – from international law and practice, the behaviour of the global economy, transnational business and financial activity, crimes, and, with the development of information technology, communications on a global scale.

Last, and most important, I was the witness of – and a participant in – the process of drawing up a new agenda of points of global concern. Most now realise the dangers our little animal species has created for the good health of the planet, in particular the vertiginous increase in our numbers, pollution of land, water and air, consumption of resources in industrial countries, pressure on resources elsewhere, and destruction of other forms of life. I was a member of the ginger group which began the preparations for the United Nations Conference at Rio (the first meetings of the group were in the British Mission). Other obvious points were new threats to human health, in particular AIDS and now SARS, a vast increase in the numbers of refugees, and resurgence of ethnic and religious strife, the more assertive role of nongovernmental organisations, and not least an increasing polarisation of the world's rich and the world's poor.

Superpower

In some respects we seem to have reached a watershed. So far I have described the gradual, sometimes hesitant movement of the world community towards international codes of conduct and law, and willingness to cooperate in coping with global issues, whether of peace and war, or of sustainability in all its aspects. But now we have to face up to what, I suppose, was a natural consequence of the ending of the cold war in the late 1980s and early 1990s: the emergence of a single superpower – the United States – which is increasingly setting its own agenda, laws, and rules of conduct.

The process goes back to the end of the First World War. I saw some of it for myself during the years I was at the United Nations in New York. Over the 1980s the United States was an ever more grumpy and reluctant partner in international affairs. For many Americans the rest of the world seemed a long way away, and the US interest in international management was in sharp decline. More than ever the criterion for any action was national interest rather than global interest.

These tendencies have become much clearer in the Administration of President Bush Junior. The way in which the United States with British support, tried to bully the Security Council into endorsing a war against Iraq, and then, having failed, launched it all the same, is present in all our minds. Now the same countries are trying to legitimise the outcomes. Already unilateralism had taken over in Washington. John Major had to twist President Bush Senior's arm to get him to the Rio Conference in 1992; but no one could persuade President Bush Junior to go to the Johannesburg Conference ten years later. His Secretary of State got pretty rough treatment as a result.

The story is the same in other fields. The United States withdrew unilaterally from the Anti Ballistic Missile Treaty; it failed to ratify the Biodiversity Convention or to accept the Biosafety Protocol; it refused to join the International Criminal Court (maintaining somehow that Americans were different from everyone else); it failed to ratify the UN Convention on the Rights of the Child; and it refused to accept a new protocol to the Biological and Toxic Weapons Convention.

The attitude of the Administration towards climate change aroused particular indignation elsewhere. The science is not now in question. Nor are the potential hazards for the world as a whole, including the United States. There is a marked contrast.

- On the one hand is the US scientific community which has been – and still is – to the fore in much of the research on climate change and its likely impacts worldwide. The same goes for some individual US states, and many in the US business community

- On the other is the Administration with its withdrawal from the Kyoto Protocol and negative attitude on climatic as well as other environmental issues. The non-participation of the US in the global effort on climate change is far more than a national embarrassment; indeed, it is dangerous – as was recently written by the editor of *Science* magazine.

There are of course many inconsistencies in US policies. For example, most Americans have an almost religious belief in free trade and market economics, but the Administration indulges in a wide range of subsidies and protectionist measures. It is not, of course, alone in doing so. But it has the utmost difficulty in accepting the judgements of the World Trade Organization, and is far from putting into effect what was agreed at the Doha meeting last year. Recent tariffs on steel, and subsidies to US agriculture have outraged the international community. It is now trying to force the European Union to accept agricultural products which include genetically modified organisms.

For the rest of the world, the most conspicuous feature of US foreign policy is the exertion of military power, unencumbered by much diplomacy or respect for the corpus of law and custom built up in the twentieth century. It seems strange that capitalist America should so endorse Mao Tse-tung's saying (in his *Little Red Book*) that 'political power grows out of the barrel of a gun.' Yet the United States spends more on defence and military technology than most other countries put together. Increasingly it looks like the world policeman operating under its own book of rules. The world has known superpowers before, whether they be Persia, Greece, Rome, China, Spain, France, or Britain in their day, but the power of each has always been based to some extent on bluff, and they have pushed others into redressing the balance. Imperial over-stretch was a regular feature. I expect it will be so in the future as in the past. Already the United States has an enormous and growing trade deficit, with a weakening currency, and is losing its technological superiority in most fields except defence. Its empire like all empires, will be ephemeral.

What of the future?

What of the future? Empires are fed and driven by an ever increasing need for resources. At this point the problem for the United States and the world as a whole becomes glaringly obvious. I hope that many of you will take time to read the remarkable statement published after a meeting of scientists in the four international global change research programmes at Amsterdam in July 2001. There it stated squarely that

- 'Human activities have the potential to switch the Earth's System to alternative modes of operation that may prove irreversible and less hospitable to humans and other life. The nature of changes now occurring simultaneously in the Earth's system, their magnitudes and rates of change are unprecedented. The Earth is currently operating in a no-analogue state'.
- 'The accelerating human transformation of the Earth's environment is not sustainable. Therefore the business-as-usual way of dealing with the Earth's System is *not* an option. It has to be replaced – as soon as possible – by deliberate strategies of management that sustain the Earth's environment while meeting social and economic development objectives'.

    (The Amsterdam Declaration on Global Change. Made by the International Geosphere-Biosphere Programme (IGBP), the International Human Dimensions Programme on Global Environmental

Change (IHDP), the World Climate Research Programme (WCRP) and the international biodiversity programme (DIVERSITAS) – http://www.sciconf.igbp. kva.se/Amsterdam_Declaration.html)

No wonder that Crutzen (Max-Planck-Institute for Chemistry, D-55020 Mainz, Germany) and Stoermer (Center for Great Lakes and Aquatic Sciences, University of Michigan, USA) have labelled the present epoch since the beginning of the industrial revolution as the Anthropocene (see http://www.mpch-mainz.mpg.de.de/ air/anthropocene/Text.html). It carries with it many implications: among them the paramount need for greater global cooperation, and risks of conflict arising from competition for resources.

Two major global themes

Concern about resources is the more important of the two major global themes that have emerged in the last twenty years. The other relates to how humanity consequently divides these resources and the increasing globalisation of world trade. At present about 20 per cent of the world's people consume between 70 per cent and 80 per cent of its resources. The dividing line between rich and poor is not only between countries but also within them. Even in India and China, the rift is between globalised rich and the localised poor. There has been debate whether globalisation has exacerbated this divide. Successive UNDP Human Development Reports, especially that of 1999, suggest that it has. As the UN Secretary-General well said in assessing progress on the Millennium Development Goals

> There is no autopilot, there is no magic of the market place, no rising tide of the global economy that will lift all boats,

guaranteeing that all goals will be reached by 2015.
(see http://www.hri.org/news/world/undh/2003/03-11-06.undh.html)

Clearly we are talking about global problems that require global solutions, and here the United Nations is key. Otherwise risks of conflict arising from them – for example over water – greatly increase. Multilateral approaches to sustainability have a long history which can be split into three phases.

Three phases

The first phase was between the UN Conference on the Human Environment at Stockholm in 1972 and that on Environment and Development at Rio in 1992. This phase led to: the creation of the United Nations Environment Programme (UNEP) in 1973; two World Climate Conferences in 1979 and 1990; and the report of the Brundtland Commission on Environment and Development of 1987.

The second phase was between 1992 and 2001. The achievements of the Rio Conference included a declaration containing three important principles: that the polluter should pay; that the often misunderstood precautionary principle should be more widely applied; and that environmental considerations should be at the centres of decision-making. Then there were legally binding Conventions on Climate Change and Biological Diversity and later Desertification which have been followed by subsequent Conferences of the Parties. There was Agenda 21, or a voluminous list of action points for this century. The UN Commission on Sustainable Development was created. Finally it was agreed to revise World Bank lending and to reformulate the Global Environmental Facility.

The third phase takes us to where we are today. Since Rio, the Conventions then created have mostly been ratified, and there have been several Conferences of the Parties. But generally the results have been disappointing. Reports prepared for the Johannesburg Conference indicated that most global environmental problems are getting worse.

Johannesburg

What of Johannesburg? Did global governance attain a new level of maturity? The encompassing theme should have been how to exercise human responsibility for the state of the planet in our own interest as well as that of other creatures in the global ecosystem. The result was well described by Geoffrey Lean, the doyen of British environmental journalists: although the summit was not a disaster, it did represent missed opportunities. The political declaration said little new, and was a triumph of repackaging. As for the Plan of Implementation, you will have your views on its value and only time will tell its true worth. Of course there were good points, but it is an apt description to say that there were many trees but little wood.

At Johannesburg, global problems were sold short and the United States was not alone in contributing to the result.

Four main handicaps

If we are at a watershed, some, not least in this country, have been inclined to blame the United Nations for what has happened, or not happened, at the UN decision-making bodies in New York. This is not only unjust but also simply wrong. In my view the United Nations and its institutions suffer from four main handicaps. Until recently, in spite of recent shortcomings, the UN system has had almost excessive political credibility. Far more responsibility is loaded on it than it can possibly carry. Secondly, the tasks it is given are often confused or imprecise, not least because member states themselves do not know how to cope with them. Thirdly, it is not given the financial and other resources it needs to function effectively. The reason it did not succeed in Kosovo was that it did not have anything like sufficient resources. Lastly, it is not allowed to carry through necessary internal changes and reforms.

Wanting more

There is a curious and unbridged gap between the often repeated wish of governments, expressed in the Security Council, the General Assembly and elsewhere, for the United Nations to defend international order, fulfil its obligations under the Charter, and take on new responsibilities; and the means – political, financial and administrative – by which it could do so. Governments often blame the United Nations for failures. More legitimately the United Nations blames governments.

Even though many governments say they want or expect more of the United Nations, and say they accept the substance of a new global agenda, most also want to hold on to their sovereignty – and money – as long as possible, and in some cases keep the United Nations from interfering in their affairs. In short governments lack the political will to tackle the issues themselves and are even less willing to let the United Nations take a lead for them.

This all sounds very gloomy. But perhaps current circumstances may oblige governments to do what they were reluctant even to think about before. Certainly the value of the United Nations has been underlined by current efforts to give it what both President Bush and Prime Minister Blair said would be a 'vital role' in the reconstruction of Iraq. What it means remains to be seen. Clare Short's resignation (in May 2003) showed what she thought of the latest Anglo-American draft resolution (May 2003) before the Security Council. All sides at least recognise that the issue needs explicit political and financial support from all members in or out of the Security Council. Others would go still further, and give the United Nations the central role in negotiating at long last a settlement over Palestine.

As for the role of the United Nations and its agencies in dealing with the major issues of sustainability, climate change and protection of the environment, there is simply no other place or institution capable of organising and promoting planetary action. Conferences of the Parties to such global agreements as the Kyoto Protocol and the Convention on Biological Diversity will continue and the UN Secretary-General has asked the UN Development Programme to monitor the Johannesburg and Monterrey targets and the Millennium Development Goals. During the eleventh meeting of the UN Commission on Sustainable Development, a working cycle was established for the review of the Johannesburg targets.

Priorities

The Johannesburg Conference may have been a failure, but the problems it failed to deal with will not go away. They will be of gathering importance in the future. My own priorities are that we need to

- look again at economics, and the way we measure wealth, welfare and human progress in terms of the Earth's good health

- redefine development, and give more respect to the different needs – and possibilities – of different countries
- apply the principles of common but differentiated responsibility, accepting that industrial countries have much bigger responsibilities, and above all should give the example in their domestic policies. Getting rid of perverse subsidies would be a good start
- underline the need for partnerships at all levels: governments, business, local communities, and establish new guidelines and codes of conduct. For example, tensions over water can lead to compromise rather than conflict.

In some respects, this is happening already. Governments were not the only people meeting in Johannesburg though others received little media attention. The work of non-governmental organisations of all kinds, judges, business and industry, local and regional authorities may have been less tangible but in the long run it may prove to have been more significant.

Here the multilateral approach is the only approach. Wars must not be allowed to crowd out, even temporarily, the need to think about the big issues and work together in trying to resolve them. An enormous amount needs to be done. If the United Nations did not exist, we would have to invent it.

More than an institution

But it is more than an institution; it is an ideal. We need to hold on to the uplifting idea of the United Nations as the magic world in which humankind is 'one'. Here symbols are vital. Seen from space as a passenger in the solar system, the Earth is a tiny bright dot, or from closer to it, the blue water world. No matter that the myth does not always correspond with the reality, nor that its principles and standards are not always observed. The truth behind any set of myths, principles and standards is acceptance of aspirations held in common. That is the goal of multilateralism and the ultimate strength of the United Nations. We damage it at our peril.

PROSECUTING WAR CRIMINALS

Judge Richard Goldstone

Lecture delivered on 9 November 2003

I was delighted to get an invitation from Brian Walker to address a meeting of the Religious Society of Friends in Kendal Town Hall. I was particularly pleased for two reasons. The first is that for many years I have admired the philosophy and the work of the Quakers and the second, let me confess, I could not resist an invitation to come to the Lake District. I have always wanted to come and have never had the time or the opportunity. It has been a wonderful twenty-four hours in this lovely part of the world.

What I propose to do is give you some of the history of the Law of War, so that you can understand the tools – the laws both domestic and international – that are available to us when we seek to prosecute war criminals. I will discuss the development of Humanitarian Law and universal jurisdiction, the work of the United Nations and the War Crimes Tribunals, and I will say a little about the International Criminal Court.

Humanitarian law and universal jurisdiction

The history of the Law of War, as it used to be called – it is now called International Humanitarian Law, or simply

Humanitarian Law – goes back many thousands of years. One finds references to elementary aspects of the Law of War in Chinese and Indian writings of at least a thousand years ago – even two to three thousand years ago. The idea was to have reciprocity: if you treat my people who you capture on the battlefield humanely, I will reciprocate and do the same in respect of your citizens; but let me warn you, if you treat my captured people badly, do not expect any better treatment of yours. Thus it was very much a reciprocal arrangement, and the Law of War in its modern guise continued in that tradition.

The modern Law of War began, of course, as a result of the work of the International Committee of the Red Cross in the nineteenth century. Henry Dunant, a wealthy Swiss businessman, was horrified at the way injured soldiers were left to die in agony on the fields of Solferino in Italy, and he decided to do something about it. I think we should remember that it was one person who founded the International Committee of the Red Cross: it is amazing what leadership can do and what a difference one person can make. It is interesting that the very first recipient of the Nobel Peace Prize was Henry Dunant, in response to the work of the International Committee of the Red Cross.

International Law generally deals with *when* it is legal to make war, but Humanitarian Law, as developed by the Red Cross, deals with the *way* in which wars should be fought. Thus it does not deal with whether war should be declared, or whether a war is lawful. The analogy that I always like using comes from the so-called sport of boxing: the Queensberry Rules apply only once the bell has been rung and two men – I am afraid to say these days even women – try to knock each other senseless. The Queensberry Rules do not refer to, nor do they have any-thing to do with, the morality or legality of the sport of boxing; they are simply triggered by the bell ringing to indicate the first round. The Law of War is similar. This confuses many people – they wonder why the Law of War does not outlaw war. It does not outlaw war because it is only triggered *when* the war begins. I think that is an important aspect to bear in mind.

Historically, the Law of War recognised nations rather than individuals. Before the Second World War, and before the United Nations system, there was no such thing as an international court recognising individual human beings – the World Court was under the League of Nations, which recognised only governments – nor were individuals recognised as the subject matter of International Law. 'Human Rights' were matters for governments to adhere to or to violate; it was not the business of the international community. That, of course, changed in response to the terrible war crimes committed by the Nazis. Humankind was so horrified, and the consciences of decent people so disturbed that views on law began to change. International leaders recognised that individual human beings should indeed be given recognition. Thus, the first reference to human rights in an international instrument of law is in the Charter of the United Nations. Hot on the heels of the Charter came the Universal Declaration of Human Rights, which was neither an international treaty, nor a law; it was an aspiration which, happily, spawned more binding international human rights conventions in the 1960s and after.

The trigger for recognising individuals in International Law was Nuremberg. The Nuremberg Tribunal was set up by the four victorious powers, in what was called the 'London Agreement', towards the end of the Second World War. The four powers decided that the Nazi leaders should be given a fair trial – fair certainly by the standards of the 1940s and early 1950s – but the laws that were used were found to be wanting. The law is always retroactive. For example, as ways of doing business change with the use of the Internet, so the laws of banking have to change. The Law of War is similarly retroactive. After each great war the Geneva Conventions have been updated. They had to be updated after the First World War because nobody had contemplated air war – there was no such thing when the first laws were drafted in the nineteenth century. After the Second World War they had to be updated: the four Geneva Conventions with us today date from 1949, with two optional protocols updating them in 1977.

So, new laws were needed to prosecute the Nazis. It was decided to add to the jurisdiction of the Nuremberg Tribunal what were called, 'Crimes against Humanity'. Though such crimes had been referred to by academics between the two great wars, there had never been such a thing in the legal lexicon. They were recognised for the first time in charges laid against the Nazi leaders – amongst other crimes. Recognition of crimes against humanity was the key that opened a Pandora's box. Firstly, it demonstrated that some crimes are so huge, and are so horrible, that they are crimes not only against the immediate victims themselves; they are crimes not even only against the country – and its people – where the crime was committed; they are crimes truly against all of humankind. Secondly, it introduced universal jurisdiction, for if these are crimes against all people in the world, the courts of any country, no matter how remote from the scene of the crime, have jurisdiction to bring such a person to justice and, if found guilty, to punish them.

The idea of universal jurisdiction was not completely new. For many hundreds of years, pirates have attracted universal jurisdiction: they can be put on trial in any court in the world, no matter where their act of piracy took place. This legal situation arose out of necessity – since pirates do not commit their crimes on land, they do not commit their crimes in the jurisdiction of any one court. Unless *all* courts have jurisdiction, they would be given an effective amnesty. So universal jurisdiction was recognised for pirates. But as a result of the holocaust, and the other terrible crimes committed by the Nazis in the Second World War, International Law recognised the principal of universal jurisdiction in respect of war crimes.

Interestingly, the Genocide Convention, which followed Nuremberg in 1948, did not incorporate universal jurisdiction. The Genocide Convention did three things. Firstly, it defined this most horrible of crimes, the crime that requires the mental intent of wiping out a whole people or part of a people. Indeed, they had to invent a new word for a genocide, because nobody had ever thought of a crime of that magnitude. It had never entered any sane person's mind before the Second World War that anybody would wipe out a people, and although it had happened with the Armenians at the end of the First World War, there had never been a law in reaction to it. Secondly, the Genocide Convention said that the crime of genocide should be charged in domestic courts; in other words, a country should put on trial any of its citizens (or people within its borders) who commit genocide. Thirdly, however, the Convention goes on to say that a person suspected of committing genocide could also be charged by an international court. That is very interesting: in the Genocide Convention, which the United Nations passed unanimously on the 11 December 1948 – the day after the Universal Declaration of Human Rights – UN members realised and hoped that in the not too distant future there would be an international criminal court. But it was wishful thinking in 1948. It was almost half a century before the first international criminal court was set up by the United Nations, for the former Yugoslavia.

The first use in International Law of universal jurisdiction was, in fact, in the Geneva Conventions of 1949. As I have said, the Geneva Conventions had to be updated: the drafters and the plenipotentiaries who met in Geneva in 1949 realised that here, too, new war crimes needed to be recognised. They defined a new species of crime called 'grave breaches of the Geneva Conventions': the worst war crimes of all. They went on to hold that all countries that ratified the Geneva Conventions – today that is almost every nation of the world – have a duty to prosecute anybody suspected of having committed a grave breach of the Geneva Conventions. Further, they said that if a country cannot or will not prosecute and punish somebody committing a grave breach, that country has an obligation to hand the person over to a country that is willing and able to do so. Thus universal jurisdiction was for the first time recognised and made obligatory on all countries ratifying the Conventions.

The next use of universal jurisdiction, interestingly for me, was in respect of apartheid in South Africa. In 1973 the United Nations passed a convention that declared apartheid to be a crime against humanity, almost a completing of a circle between Nuremberg and apartheid in 1973. Universal jurisdiction was conferred by the United Nations Convention: it provided that any country ratifying the Apartheid Convention should bring to justice in their courts people guilty of the crime of apartheid, even though it was committed in South Africa. Unfortunately, neither Britain nor any other of the leading western nations ratified that convention; had they done so, they would have been obliged to arrest South African ambassadors, ministers – and probably business men and women who visited London to do very lucrative trade – and charge them with the crime of apartheid. It was predominantly African and Asian countries that ratified the Convention, and they were not very important to apartheid leaders or business people at that time. It is a matter for thought: had this convention been taken seriously by European and North American countries, and had South African politicians, diplomats and business people been unable to travel for fear of arrest, I have little doubt that apartheid would have died a good decade before it did. Sadly, that was not the thinking in the major capitals in those days, certainly not in the western world. So although there was recognition of universal jurisdiction in the convention, there was never, to my knowledge, a single case of universal jurisdiction being used against a person suspected of committing the crime of apartheid.

Universal jurisdiction was next used in 1984 in the Torture Convention. This was the convention that led to the arrest in England of General Pinochet when he was receiving medical treatment in a London clinic. And that, of course, started a whole new ball game. Many other oppressive dictators around the world began to have problems travelling. I remember reading that the former dictator of Indonesia, Soharto, cancelled medical treatment in Germany because he feared that a warrant of arrest under the Torture Convention might be awaiting him. Soon after the Pinochet affair, the dictator of Ethiopia had to flee South Africa, where he was receiving medical treatment, because Human Rights Watch in New York publicised that he was there. He feared arrest, and there have been many others in his position. It is fascinating that these oppressive dictators, who care nothing for the lives of the people under their care, always seek for themselves the best medical treatment; and it is always medical treatment that they have to run away from for fear of arrest. They also like holidays abroad and I think many former dictators – and present dictators – are now having to get both their medical treatment and their vacations at home to a much greater extent. That is a good thing, maybe not for travel agents, but I think for the world it is probably a healthy development.

The next use of universal jurisdiction was in the United Nations resolution that made provision for the War Crimes Tribunals for the former Yugoslavia and Rwanda. The United Nations Security Council assumed the right to create universal jurisdiction: suspects can be arrested under that statute wherever they may be found, and the Yugoslavia Tribunal has jurisdiction over crimes committed in any of the states of the former Yugoslavia. These crimes can be tried in The Hague – far from where the crimes were committed. A similar situation arose with regard to Rwanda: even if people who planned to commit the genocide in Rwanda in 1994 were subsequently found in Kenya or Uganda, they would be subject to justice in the War Crimes Tribunal sitting in Arusha, in Northern Tanzania.

One sees, then, the growing use of universal jurisdiction. Indeed, in the sixteen international conventions dealing with terrorism there is in all of them the use of universal jurisdiction. Many people, particularly in the United States, are surprised that of those conventions, fourteen anti-date the attacks of 11 September 2001. The earliest United Nations convention dealing with the scourge of terrorism comes from the 1970s, with regard to the hijacking of aircraft, the protection of international diplomats taken as hostages, the piracy of civilian ships, and so forth. There is in fact a plethora of United Nations conventions dealing with acts of terrorism, even in the absence of an agreed definition of terrorism within the international community.

As international use of universal jurisdiction increased, so too did domestic use. Famously, the Belgian parliament and judges took it upon themselves to give their courts the power to arrest and put on trial anybody committing war crimes, even if they had no connection with Belgium. They were not alone in this – there were other European countries with the same idea – but Belgium introduced it. This has now of course been amended by the Belgian parliament under threat from Washington, but it shows that there are various ways to deal with war criminals: international courts and domestic courts. Thus we in the international community are always grappling with two difficult questions: which are the appropriate courts, and what are the appropriate methods to deal with war criminals?

Added to development in international justice in regard to war crimes, was the growth of the idea of Humanitarian Intervention. It certainly came to the fore in respect of Kosovo. Humanitarian Intervention involves the use of military force, if necessary, to protect the lives of innocent civilians. Some very difficult questions obviously arose for pacifist organisations in consequence of Kosovo, because here was a case where I do not think anybody could question the motives of the NATO nations. The NATO members intervened in Kosovo for one reason only, and that was to protect the lives of innocent Albanian Muslim people who lived in this province of Serbia. There was no ulterior motive, there was no land, there was no oil, there was no trade; there was no interest at all for the United States, the United Kingdom, or any of the other NATO nations, other than the lives and safety of the people. By the time bombing started, over a million Kosovo Albanians had already been forced from their homes into refugee status, or had become displaced persons in their own province of Kosovo.

Kosovo raised a very difficult question as to the morality of using war to protect the lives of innocent people. The Swedish prime minister set up an International Investigating Committee – of which I was a member – to look into that and other questions. Our Committee included representatives of five continents, both lawyers and non-lawyers. We came to the unanimous conclusion that the intervention in Kosovo was illegal, because it did not have Security Council authorisation, but that it was legitimate or justified by the moral and political considerations which had led to intervention. Many people had difficulty following that – some people found it an oxymoron to declare an action legitimate yet illegal – but that was the conclusion that we reached and it has, I think, been generally accepted. It was accepted by the United Nations Security Council itself. Interestingly, after the Kosovo bombing had succeeded in putting an end to the ethnic cleansing – a horrible concept – of the Kosovo Albanians, Russia proposed a resolution in the Security Council condemning the bombing. That resolution was defeated by thirteen votes to two, which was a very strong *expo facto* justification, or acceptance at its lowest, of the NATO action in Kosovo.

The Kosovo Commission set certain thresholds. You see, the problem with unilateral action, or action without the Security Council, is: who is to be the judge? In this case, it was the NATO powers – it was the democracies of Western Europe and North America – that took the decision; and you and I can probably live with those governments taking that sort of decision, at least some of the time. But if they have the right to take those sorts of decisions, other governments in less democratic parts of the world are also free, and who are we to say, 'what right have you to take that decision without the Security Council?' Of course, this was exacerbated by the war on Iraq earlier this year (2003), when one nation, maybe two, effectively decided to make war on Saddam Hussein's Iraq: unilateral action without the Security Council. I must say – having been a party to the 'illegal but legitimate' conclusion on Kosovo – that to my horror, some leaders in London and in Washington tried to use the idea of 'illegal but legitimate' intervention to justify the war on Iraq. But, of course, what a huge difference there is between the motivation for the war on Sadaam Hussein, and that in respect of Kosovo. Some leaders said, 'we are making this war to protect the people of Iraq,' but of course it simply was not true; it was a bad excuse that was not persisted in, and it was not persisted in because the people of Iraq did *not* welcome the United States or even the United Kingdom troops waving stars and stripes or union jacks. It was not humanitarian intervention at all.

One sees, then, a growing need for more definition, a need to look at whether International Law is coping. I do not think that International Law or any other law should be put above change or scrutiny, though it must not be changed simply for the sake of change. Certainly, a number of bodies, including the International Committee of the Red Cross, are debating whether, in the face of international terrorism and the use of modern technology by a very few people, laws need to be changed.

United Nations and the War Crimes Tribunals

I will now say something of the difficulties and successes I have experienced through my work with the United Nations War Crimes Tribunals. The Tribunals got under way in a very slow and unsatisfactory fashion. My own appointment is possibly the best illustration of the problems. It came about in this way. The Security Council set up the Yugoslavia Tribunal in May of 1993, and the judges were selected – through the interaction of the Security Council and the General Assembly – in September and October of the same year. Under statute, the Security Council has to appoint the Chief Prosecutor, and because this was regarded as being something new and important, the Security Council agreed that there would have to be consensus on their choice. Boutros Boutros-Gali was then the general secretary of the United Nations – he nominated Venezuelan Attorney General, Ramon Escobar Salom as first Chief Prosecutor. Escobar Salom was appointed unanimously, but he informed Boutros-Gali that he could not come immediately because he was busy prosecuting a former president of Venezuela for fraud; he said he could not walk out in the middle of the trial, but it would finish in January. The trial did indeed finish in January – the former president was convicted and imprisoned – and Escobar Salom arrived in The Hague as the first Prosecutor. Three days later, however, he called Boutros-Gali to tell him that he had accepted an invitation to become the minister of home affairs in Venezuela and was resigning as Prosecutor.

It was now January of 1994, some seven months had passed since the Tribunal had been set up, and there were eleven frustrated, angry judges with no work to do in The Hague. Between January and June of 1994, Boutros-Gali nominated eight people to be Prosecutor. Each one was vetoed by members of the Security Council. Russia vetoed five who came from NATO countries. The United States put up one of their people, an academic who happens to be a Muslim, and the United Kingdom vetoed him. That decision angered Muslim nations because they thought, rightly or wrongly, that the United Kingdom did not want a Muslim in that position. There were good grounds for having such a view with regard to the religious make-up of the Balkans. Then, when the United Kingdom put up a Scottish lawyer, the Muslim countries vetoed him to punish the United Kingdom. One of the nominees put up by Boutros-Gali was Soli Sorabjee, the Attorney General of India, who would have made an outstanding Prosecutor; unfortunately, Pakistan – which had a seat on the Security Council – vetoed the idea of an Indian holding that position. Imagine the effects, I might say, on the victims. The victims of most terrible war crimes were buoyed-up when the Security Council set up the Tribunal: they thought, *somebody is taking notice of our victimisation*. Then there was no prosecutor for fifteen months because of political games, and there *were* political games being played by the members of the Security Council.

This, then, was the position in June of 1994, when a bright French judge suggested to the Italian President of the Tribunal that if they could find somebody with the support of Nelson Mandela, it would be impossible in the middle of 1994 for anybody to veto him or her in the Security Council. So they came to me. I was not particularly interested for good reasons. I knew nothing about Humanitarian Law and I was not an international lawyer. I had never prosecuted in my life, nor did I know anything about the Balkans. When the invitation came from Judge Cassese, I had no intention at all of taking it. But then two things happened; two important people in my life thought differently. One was Nelson Mandela, who said that it was very important I should do this – the War Crimes Tribunal was important and it was the first international position offered to a South African after our democratic election in the middle of 1994. He put a great deal of pressure on me, and he had as his great ally my wife, who thought it was a good idea to get out of South Africa for a couple of years as we had lived under heavy police security. I really had no way of resisting a combination of Nelson Mandela and my wife, so I ended up taking the position. But you can see behind this process the real political games that went on, and the reason why, in my view, War Crimes Tribunals in International Courts should not be controlled by politicians. They are simply not going to work. If those sorts of games are also the manner in which decisions are taken as to where war crimes should or should not be investigated, then in my view, and I say it in all seriousness, rather do not have an International Criminal Court at all.

International Criminal Court

In any event, the Tribunals began and I was fortunate in having outstanding advisors, and a wonderful Deputy Prosecutor from Australia, Graham Blewitt, without whom none of it would have happened. Tremendous support came from the United States in the beginning. Of course, it is ironic now, but without the United States' economic, financial and political help, the Yugoslavia Tribunal would never have got off its feet; and, having got off its feet, would never have been as successful as it was. The same can be said for the Rwanda Tribunals. We did have successes. No human institution has only successes and no failures, but the Yugoslavia and Rwanda Tribunals have been successful in two important areas in my view. One is that they have proved without any question that an International Criminal Court can work and can put on fair trials. I have heard no serious criticism relating to the fairness of the procedures adopted in The Hague or Arusha Tribunals. Second, and perhaps as important, is the fact that advances have been made in Humanitarian Law because of those Courts. Indeed, until those Courts began functioning the wonderful body of Humanitarian Law, which the International Committee of the Red Cross has been responsible for building-up over almost one and a half centuries, was never used; and if the law is not used it stagnates, it becomes worth little more than the paper on which it is written. But with the use of it in the Yugoslavia and Rwanda Tribunals the law advanced. For example, systematic mass rape became recognised for the first time as a war crime: though it was not referred to in any of the laws (which had been drafted by men, by the way, and I think that is the reason for it), rape has been held in the Rwanda tribunal in certain circumstances to constitute genocide. So there has been a huge advance in the law.

These successes were sufficient to galvanise the movement towards a permanent International Criminal Court. Again, it is ironic that it was the United States which led that movement. It was the United States which encouraged the Secretary-General of the United Nations to call the meeting in Rome in June and July of 1998 for an agreement on the International Criminal Court. What changed, and it was a tragedy, was that the United States, under pressure from its own military, performed an about-turn. Instead of being the leading nation in favour of the International Criminal Court, the United States became an opponent; and when it came to the vote in Rome, the United States joined only six other countries, including Syria, China, Qatar, Yemen and Israel, in opposing the Rome Statute. During the Clinton administration, they were not going to take active steps to undermine the International Criminal Court; and they signed, though they had no intention of ratifying the Rome Statute. But that, of course, has changed. When the Bush administration came into power, President Bush gave notice to the Secretary-General that he was un-signing what President Clinton had signed, and that he was not going to sit by: his administration was going to take active steps to undermine the infant International Criminal Court.

Since then, the judges have been elected, and ninety-two countries have ratified the Rome Statute, so there is a critical mass of nations, including every member of the European Union, and certainly a strong majority of Commonwealth countries. But 'the jury is out'. I do not know whether that Institution is going to be successful in the face of opposition from the world's sole superpower. I am not un-optimistic. They have appointed an outstanding and very experienced Argentinian Prosecutor, Luis Moreno-Ocampo, who has built up a wonderful staff. He has already indicated publicly that the first investigations will be into terrible war crimes committed in the Democratic Republic of the Congo, a situation crying out for investigation. It is also a sensible place to start, politically; whether the decision was taken with that in mind I do not know – and if I did know I would not discuss it – but it is perhaps a good thing that the first investigations will be in a part of the world that the United States does not feel particularly threatened by. If it was in the Middle

East, I think it would be a very different situation. Incidentally, since none of the relevant countries have ratified the Rome Treaty, the International Criminal Court does not in fact have jurisdiction over any war crimes committed in the Middle East.

I am an optimist and I have no doubt that there is a need, a crying need, for an International Criminal Court if war criminals are going to be put on trial. Let me end by saying that the most important aspect of international law – and I have referred to them indirectly already – are the victims. They are always forgotten. Politicians seem to put them at the bottom of the agenda if they appear on it at all – when it came to those vetoes in the Security Council, nobody gave a thought to the victims. The victims are always people who are far away from your shores, people who look different to you, and who do not, therefore, seem to evoke the sympathy or even the interest of many people. One sees it even now in this present Iraq war (2003): newspapers in the United States and in the United Kingdom are very precise about the number of their people who have been killed, yet I have not even seen estimates of the number of Iraqis, innocent Iraqis, who have been killed in this war. They simply drop off the agenda because they do not matter. I think this explains, also, how some of the horrors of war can be committed: because certain people do not seem to evoke our sympathy, they are somehow less worthy than our own. I do not think that some of these war crimes would be committed if these people are regarded as our equal and as deserving of equal rights.

What are the issues?

What, then, are the issues facing us in the twenty-first century? As I have said, I am an optimist, but I am not a great optimist about stopping war. The twentieth century was a very bloody one. One thing I do know is that if war criminals are seriously hunted down and punished it can act as a deterrent. It will not work in all cases, but in some cases it will. It is like any criminal justice system, no different from that of your own country: the more efficient the legal justice system, the lower the crime rate; the less efficient the legal justice system, the higher the crime rate. I can see it being no different in the international community. If would-be war criminals truly feared arrest and punishment some of them would think twice. I will give one illustration in conclusion. In all of the three recent wars fought by NATO and/or the United States – in Kosovo, Afghanistan, and Iraq – great care has been taken to avoid civilian deaths. Kosovo was remarkable: in seventy-eight days of bombing, fewer than two thousand people were killed; quite remarkable having regard to the figures of 10:1 (the ratio of civilian deaths to deaths of members of the armed forces) in virtually every other war since the Second World War. Afghanistan was the same, to a lesser extent; there, daily statements were made by the United States' President and military leaders, saying 'we are taking steps to protect innocent civilians, we are applying the Geneva Conventions.' And so too, in Iraq, though mistakes and wrong decisions may have been made.

Were it not for War Crimes Tribunals and the publicity given to war crimes, I do not believe there would have been that attitude on the part of the western nations with regard to the protection of civilians. Of course, it is not great comfort, because it is the oppressive dictators, not the democratic countries that one worries about; but, certainly, in other wars, the democracies did not think twice about killing innocent civilians. In Vietnam 90% of the war dead were civilians, in Korea 54%. There was no thought given when dropping the atom bomb on Hiroshima. This is a change and it is a change that I have no doubt has been brought about by the existence of the War Crimes

Tribunals, and the fear that leaders in the western world – be they political or military leaders – have of being branded as war criminals. Public opinion is also changing and public opinion is important. That is the importance of groups like this, because your voices *are* heard. It is not only the Henry Dunants who make a difference – all of us, in our private lives and in our public lives, can make a difference.

THE MINDS OF LEADERS: DE-LINKING WAR AND VIOLENCE

Dr Christopher Williams and Yun-Joo Lee

Commissioned by *Preparing for Peace* in 2003

Introduction

War is made in the minds of men, concluded the founders of
the UN. But it is made in the minds of particular 'men' –
those who are leaders. If the idea of war as a political force
is to change, the minds of those with power must change.
We cannot make war totally unthinkable. It has been
invented, so it will always be thinkable. But how is it is
possible to create a context in which war is unthinkable
because it is not perceived as a feasible, rational or legitimate political act by those with power?

The first part of this paper outlines familiar understand-
ings of the evolutionary/biological drivers of violence and
aggression, but also the argument that this alone does not
create war. It then establishes that war is made by leaders.
Despite this, leadership theory has been ignored, yet
straightforward conceptual frameworks are relevant and
applicable. The discussion then identifies contexts in
which war seems to have been made less thinkable.
Regionalisation is central, but there are other aspects: cosmopolitanism, nuclear deterrence, and the self-perception
and *persona* of leaders. North Korea is then used as a case

study, which pulls together many of the themes of the paper. Leaders 'invent' war through linking and de-linking functions, circumstances and ideas, and naming events and concepts, in a way that suits their personal ambitions. Therefore in conclusion, 're-linking' strategies are identified, which can frame the work of civil society organisations and progressive leaders who aim to make war less thinkable. It can provide the means to de-link war from violence.

The term 'war' is used broadly throughout this discussion to include organised aggression and violence between states or other significant political actors. But there is no assumption that legitimate defence and humanitarian intervention should be precluded, nor that the use of force is morally wrong. Arguably, small-scale conflict acts like intermittent bush-fires or earthquakes[i], and may prevent total destruction. Large-scale political violence is now wrong through self-interest. We have become too good at war, and it now amounts to potential suicide. Harm caused by war has escalated exponentially, and this is not just because technology has created weapons of mass destruction. The genocide in Rwanda resulted from small handheld weapons, often no more than knives. It was information technologies that permitted aggression to be organised and promoted on a genocidal scale.

Asymmetrical war provides the new dimension. The obvious example seems to be the US. Decades of war in the form of aggressive foreign policy has become suicidal because those who see themselves as victims, rightly or wrongly,[ii] can now find novel ways of employing technology to retaliate.[iii] Retaliation is equally suicidal. No expense will be spared to eliminate the apparent aggressors – and anyone else who happens to be in the way. Any act of political violence now has the potential for self-destruction, and that is a form of madness which rational self-interested people will seek to prevent. In the future, the main weapon of mass destruction will be the human mind, particularly the minds of leaders, and that is where prevention must start.

1. Made in the minds of 'men'

1.1. The evolutionary/biological drivers

In his book *Straw Dogs*, philosopher John Gray argues that humans are simply another kind of animal, war is a game, and those who play it greatly enjoy it.[iv] At an interpersonal level, the main drivers of competition and aggression are evolutionary and biological,[v] and include status, possessions, group loyalties and a hunting instinct. These motivations are now not a declared purpose or reason of war, but they remain a means to inspire men to fight. Steven Pinker shows that one of the goals of tribal raiding was men's desire to capture women,[vi] and anthropologists point to social benefits such as increasing genetic diversity and exchanging ideas and culture.[vii] Traditional male 'rights' over women in warfare are even noted and sanctioned in the Bible.

> And the children of Israel took all the women of Midian captives ... And Moses said unto them, Have ye saved all the women alive? ... kill every woman that hath known man by lying with him. But all the women children, that have not known a man by lying with him, keep alive for yourselves. (Numbers 31:9,15,17,18 King James Version)

Pinker points out that rape remains one of the hidden rewards of war for men. Proposals for an international convention to make political and military leaders responsible if their troops engage in systematic rape may do more to make war unthinkable than conventions about weapons of mass destruction.

These evolutionary/biological drivers clearly persist in modern humans. But Pinker reminds us that fighting is not rational evolutionary behaviour, *if* combatants recognise that the likelihood is death or injury. The difficulty is that the recognition of the threat usually comes too late or is masked by technology or tactics by military and political leaders. He also argues that humans engage in organised conflict because of our mental 'enforcement calculator' – we can contrive enforcement systems for punishing deserters and cowardice, and for rewarding bravery.

Pinker might have added another of his insights – that evolution has programmed us to dislike being cheated. Getting people to fight often entails deception and violence by leaders against their own group. In evolutionary terms, a leader is an extension of the head of a family – a trusted life-maker and breadwinner. So this form of deception and self-harm raises strong emotions, and is hidden by despots. Making the unseen seen, is a significant strategy for making war unthinkable.

1.2 Inventing war

In 1940, anthropologist Margaret Mead wrote a paper called 'Warfare is only an invention'.[viii] War is learned, she argued. It is a social invention like writing or marriage, and should be viewed as distinct from interpersonal violence and aggression, which have evolutionary/biological roots. At certain times societies believe that their history proposes that war is the right response to a particular set of circumstances. It seems to follow that if we can change that perception of tradition, the likelihood of war would be diminished.

But war is more than an anonymous social invention. It cannot be achieved just by a population working in an unconscious harmony. Societies have to be persuaded to believe that their history proposes that war is a necessary and viable option. This is achieved by powerful individuals who do the 'inventing' and utilise the desire and ability of human beings to follow. Social inventions arise through linking (or conflating) to create a concept. Marriage in the west has been invented by religious and political leaders by conflating functions, circumstances and ideas, such as weddings, love, co-habitation, sexual ethics, birth, child-rearing, and family. Yet there are many examples of marriage or its equivalent occurring in other configurations. Like marriage, 'war' can be de-linked to change the nature of the concept.

Gray, Pinker and Mead identify the two factors that make war thinkable – the awareness of evolutionary/biological drivers, and the knowledge that these can be harnessed through societal action to achieve mass violence. This is broadly accepted, but writers rarely go further and point out that this would not happen without power elites. It is leaders who can manipulate our primitive instincts to fight, can mask the risks of fighting, and can create enforcement systems. It is leaders who set goals, plan, strategise and arrange for the mass production and accumulation of weapons.

1.3 Leading and following

If we are looking for the roots of war – evolutionary or social – the human ability to lead and follow are arguably the most significant reasons. Without those human abilities, aggression would involve little more than punch-ups and skirmishes. In *The Anatomy of Human Destructiveness*, Eric Fromm identifies the instinct to follow as crucial. 'Conformist aggression', as he terms it, 'comprises various acts of aggression that are performed not because the aggressor is driven by the desire to destroy, but because he [sic] is told to do so and considers it his duty to obey orders.' He continues in relation to World War Two, 'The soldier had traditionally been made to feel that to obey his leaders was a moral and religious obligation for the fulfillment of which he should be ready to pay with his life.' He concludes that 'major wars in modern times and most wars between the states of antiquity were not caused by dammed-up aggression, but by instrumental aggression of the military and political elites.' In support he quotes a study by Q. Wright,[ix] which leads him to conclude that the intensity of war 'is highest among the powerful states with a strong government and lowest among primitive man without permanent chieftainship.'[x] War would be unthinkable if uncritical obedience, unquestioning followers, and abuse of power by leaders became unthinkable.

In the legal arena, the recognition of the accountability of individual leaders for political violence stems from precedents from the Nuremberg and Tokyo trials. These were then affirmed in the Statutes of the Yugoslav and Arusha Tribunals, and that of the International Criminal Court. This marks a new era in which powerful people can be held responsible for harm, as individuals. But the new ethic goes further. It is an era in which leaders are likely to be seen as *more* culpable because of their power, and the breach of trust. And it is now well established that 'only following orders' is not a defence.[xi] The international community seems not yet to realise fully the significance of this new ethos, and its implications for the accountability of powerful people in other spheres of life.[xii]

Reflecting this ethic, there is now a broader realisation: contemporary conflicts are not fundamentally caused by phenomena described in popularist terms such as 'nationalism', 'ethnic hatred' or a 'clash of civilisations'. Such conflicts are constructed and fuelled by powerful people to serve their own ends. Fromm points out that, 'when Hitler started his attack against Poland and, thus, as a consequence triggered the Second World War, popular enthusiasm for the war was practically nil. The population, in spite of years of heavy militaristic indoctrination, showed very clearly that they were not eager to fight this war.'[xiii] Distinctions such as 'Serbs', 'Muslims', 'Croats' in the Balkans were not significant until they served a purpose for local despots. The Carnegie enquiry into the *Causes and Conduct of the Balkan Wars in 1912-13* (note the date) concluded.

> The real culprits ... are not, we repeat, the Balkan peoples ... The true culprits are those who mislead public opinion and take advantage of the people's ignorance to raise disquieting rumours ... inciting their country and consequently other countries into enmity. The real culprits are those who by interest or inclination, declaring constantly that war is inevitable, end by making it so, asserting that they are powerless to prevent it. The real culprits are those who sacrifice the general interest to their own personal interest ...[xiv]

More broadly, Mark Mazower argues

> 'Ethnic cleansing' – whether in the Balkans in 1912-13, in Anatolia in 1921-2 or in erstwhile Yugoslavia in 1991-5 – was not, then, the spontaneous eruption of primeval hatreds but the deliberate use of organised violence by paramilitary squads and army units; it represented the extreme force required by nationalists to break apart a society which was otherwise capable of ignoring the mundane fractures of class and ethnicity.'[xv]

Conclusions of this nature are common. It is curious that, although the implication of powerful individuals is clear, the word 'leader' has not appeared in such statements until very recently. But then the minds of leaders often control the discourse of history.

Bill Berkeley's book, *The graves are not yet full*, demonstrates the implication of powerful individuals very directly in relation to certain African countries. He concludes: 'Call it "tribalism", call it "nationalism", call it "fundamentalism" – the role of political leaders in fomenting civil conflicts has been the paramount civil rights issue of the post-Cold War era.'[xvi] Similarly, if less convincingly, Rubin argues that although the US has made significant contributions to regional stability, 'Arabs throughout the Middle East are constantly told by their leaders that the United States is the party responsible for Iraq's problems.' He continues, 'The basic reason for the prevalence of Arab anti-Americanism, then, is that it has been a useful tool for radical rulers … to build domestic support and pursue regional goals with no significant cost.'[xvii]

> It takes leadership, operating in a context of political upheaval and insecurity – and impunity – to translate hostility and suspicion into violent conflict.
> (Bill Berkeley, *The graves are not yet full*)[xviii]

1.4 Inventing and linking

Leaders invent war by *linking and de-linking functions, circumstances and ideas – and naming the resultant concepts and events – in ways that make war thinkable to themselves and to followers.* Discourse is central. Currently we are to fear 'Islamic terrorists', yet we were not told to fear 'Christian terrorists' in the form of the IRA. The perception of whether conflict is *between* or *within* particular social groups is manipulated. At a global level, it is hard to think of an inter-civilisational war since the Crusades, yet we are to believe that a war between civilisations is imminent and needs preventing.[xix] Arguably the main inter-civilisational 'clashes' we witness have been conceptual, cultural or in the sports arena, not on the battlefield. Whether wars are between or within defined social groups is not as clear as our leaders would like us to believe. Wars are made by leaders to justify and further their own ends, and they will construct and present seeming adversaries in the way that best suits those ends.

A view of twentieth century history that was created without the influence of powerful people, might further question the standard perceptions of whether wars are between or within particular groups. The so-called 'World Wars' were primarily between Europeans. Should we talk of 'World Wars', or the 'Christian Wars' or 'European Wars'? The Cold War was presented as between two radically different ideologies. Yet, as John Gray points out, more accurately, it was 'a family quarrel among western ideologies',[xx] with their conceptual roots in England. Ireland's quasi-religious and quasi-political leaders have fomented an ongoing and unfathomable conflict for centuries, but is it between Catholics and Protestants, or among Christians? Why was the Balkan conflict 'between' Serbs and Muslims, but not another 'European War'?

Beyond Europe, the Iran-Iraqi war can be seen as a war among Muslims, not between two nations. Even the violence between the Arabs and Jews is, from another perspective, within a Semitic group, genetically indistinguishable and with very similar cultural and legal practices – 'salem' and 'shalom' both mean peace. East Asian people have been fighting with themselves for a hundred years, yet the East Asian region is the most homogeneous in the world. Japan's colonial violence included seemingly 'international' aggression against Korea. But historically Korean and Japanese people are genetically, linguistically and culturally linked. The current Japanese Emperor has now even acknowledged the Korean ancestry of his family. The Korean War might seem to exemplify an in-group war. But the 'opposing forces' of North and South were constructed by Russia and the US. The war was started by the Soviet Union[xxi] and fought between the US and China, supported by other Cold War factions (including a manipulated UN), and played out on Korean territory at the expense of Korean people. Currently it is termed an 'international war'.[xxii] This may be terminologically correct, but is not a distinction that can be substantiated on cultural, racial, or arguably even on 'national' grounds.

Was the west responsible for constructing the idea of modern war – of linking war and violence in a way that was not known before? For example, did the Meiji rulers in Japan learn to become an aggressive expansionist force by watching the conduct of their western counterparts? Before this time, conflict in and around Japan was ritualised in the form of the Samurai, an idea that was probably imported from Korea (*sa ur ae be*). Only 8 per cent of Japanese families were Samurai, and they operated within a strict code of honour. Commoners were not allowed to carry swords, so violence was contained within this small military cadre. In 1869, the government pensioned off the Samurai. Was this to diminish violence, or to create a context in which a large national, European-style army could be created, under the control of a single leader?

One of the things that unifies an army is attack by an opposing force. Observers of the confrontation between South Korean students and the army in the 1980s remark that the adversaries were often college friends, and at first the soldiers were reluctant to confront the students. When (apparently) a few students attacked the army, this changed and the soldiers quickly engaged in a brutal confrontation. But, as may have happened in Korea, a leader can construct this effect. At the start of World War Two, Hitler staged an attack on a Silesian radio station, using Nazi officers disguised as Polish soldiers.[xxiii] The burning of the Reichstag, which was attributed to communists, has come to symbolise the phenomenon of self-attack by warring leaders. The creation of false fears or false enemies is related, even if there is no self-harm. Exposing violence and deception against one's own group, and holding leaders responsible for supposed 'retaliation', is an important means to dis-invent war.

As George Orwell proposed in *1984*, it seems that in certain circumstances political or military leaders need to construct an 'enemy' to create fear and legitimate and further their own power. In Orwellian tradition, the progeny of the September 11 attacks on the World Trade Center and Pentagon is a so-called 'War against Terrorism'. There can be no dispute that this particular 'war' is made entirely by political leaders. The enemy is an abstract noun, not an identifiable aggressor.

Having constructed an enemy, there was then need to construct 'terrorist leaders'. Of the many candidates, an obscure US-trained opportunist called Osama bin Laden was identified. Assuming that the videos and tapes are genuine, he quickly rose to fulfil a role. In return, bin Laden helped to build the image of George Bush as a seemingly great leader. In November 2002, a videotape apparently from bin Laden talked of Bush as 'the Pharoe of the age'.[xxiv] The phrase will certainly help to demonise Bush in the eyes of Arabs. The name 'Pharoah' was applied to the western-oriented Anwar Sadat by his killers twenty years ago. But doubtless George Bush would have been grateful for the vote-winning accolade. The phenomenon is not new. Erich Fromm makes this point in his description of World War 1: 'The Germans claimed that they were ... fighting for freedom by fighting the Csar; their enemies claimed that they were ... fighting for freedom by fighting the Kaiser.'[xxv]

How often has the power of 'enemy leaders' been created as much through the propaganda of adversaries than by their own actions? In December, a senior US army officer told Robert Fisk that they caught a couple of high-profile, serious al-Qa'ida leaders but they couldn't tell them what specific operations were going to take place. Although they would know that something big was planned, they would have no idea what it was.[xxvi]

The officer did not appear to question whether this level of awareness equated with men called 'high-profile' 'serious leaders'. Warring leaders need to construct one another as great 'men' – a symbiotic relationship that fuels war. Paradoxically, they use each other as a 'resource' (below, 1.5) – an entity that supports a leader in much the same way as a political party or administration.

This need to construct enemy leaders probably reflects two obvious insights by powerful aggressors. First, attacking a 'terrorist leader' is tangible and comprehensible to the public. Attacking amorphous and abstract 'terrorist cells' is not. On its own, for the US military to drop bombs on UN centres, weddings and other civilian gatherings in Afghanistan, might have led the American public to question the nature of this aggression. The US needed the excuse of trying to eliminate 'terrorist leaders' and a few itinerant clerics elevated to the status of 'Taliban leaders'. Local Afghan people would probably say that controlling their feuding warlords would have been a greater step towards ensuring their security. We all like to hate powerful people – almost any leader can easily be presented as a natural enemy of any followers.

Second, if an enemy appears leaderless, it may become very clear to the public that, while wars are made by leaders, they are fought by their followers. And it is usually not the leaders who suffer most. In ancient Greece, leaders who declared war were morally required to lead their troops into battle. Since then, leaders have cleverly de-linked themselves from the dangers of war. When a US leader takes off in *Air Force 1* or hides in a nuclear shelter, because of a threat of attack, this should be presented to the public as an act of cowardice, not leadership. During World War Two, the British royal family stayed in London and shared the dangers of bombing with their subjects.

Another trick of warring leaders is to present disagreements between elites as intrinsically disagreements between the masses. This is rarely true, and is reflected in the traditions of war. Arthur Nussbaum concludes of the 'quasi-international mores' of China during the first millennium BC, 'one stands out: the people of belligerent rulers definitely did not consider each other as enemies, and there was no discrimination against the subjects of an enemy prince.'[xxvii] More formally, the principles embodied in the Hague Conventions and the Geneva Convention affirmed that war should not harm innocent or neutral parties.[xxviii]

The ethic can evolve one stage further – as wars are made by leaders they should therefore be fought between leaders. Disputes between Korean gangs were traditionally settled through a fistfight between gang leaders, which avoided large-scale gang warfare.

Leaders present small conflicts as precipitants of a full-scale war, yet this is often untrue. They may act to limit the scale of aggression. Among East African tribes, Colin Turnbull concludes that raiding was often 'far from being an act of war, the raid acted as a mechanism for peace.'[xxix] A few warriors might die, but that settled things and avoided war for others. Eventually, the scale can become symbolic, and fought between leaders. In Arab countries, family feuds were often fought out for centuries through exchanging poetry between elites. War and violence were completely de-linked.

The central assumptions of this paper are therefore very simple. Wars are not fundamentally between social groups – nations, religions, tribes, peoples, or civilisations. Wars are constructed and presented in this way by powerful people. Wars are between leaders, real or constructed.

1.5 The academic view

The significance of powerful people seems obvious, yet in discussions about war and peace, leadership has received remarkably little analytical attention beyond the vilification of a few infamous individuals. In recognition of this, Gordon Peake asks key questions.[xxx] In conflict situations

- How do particular leaders come to power?
- Why do followers support particular types of leadership?
- Why and how do leaders maintain ongoing support during conflict?
- What are the processes of leadership decision-making?
- How can leadership be made more positive?

To these questions might be added, what is in the minds of leaders who instigate and promote conflict – what is their perception of themselves?

The absence of a holistic leadership approach to the analysis of war is evident from the indexes of standard texts on peace and security. Taking one at random, the seven-page index of *Beyond Confrontation*[xxxi] includes twenty or so immediately recognisable political leaders, power relationships are acknowledged under headings such as 'power politics' and 'authority', and context in headings such as 'Vietnam war' and 'Yalta Conference'. But there is no entry for 'leadership'. In Erich Fromm's comprehensive *Anatomy of human destructiveness*, the index similarly has no entry for 'leadership'. The six hundred and thirty pages of text includes one page on 'conformist aggression', and there are a few sentences of elaboration elsewhere. But a whole chapter analyses Hitler psychologically.[xxxii]

Standard analysis may focus on individual personalities, and may go further and assess the power relationships within administrative institutions, such as that of the Nazis. And history is almost obsessive about context and the significance of events such as the assassination of Francis Ferdinand at Sarajevo. But rarely does analysis adopt the approach of leadership studies and look at the three aspects holistically – how did particular powerful individuals behave in particular power hierarchies within particular contexts? Leadership studies have the potential to contribute more significantly to the achievement of a world without large-scale war.

Leadership can be seen as operating within identifiable but related 'parameters'.([xxxiii,xxxiv])

- the *abilities* of leaders – their mental and physical powers, including perceptive skills and character
- their *resources* – reserves that they can control and draw on for leadership support – administrations, political parties, families, networks, relationships with other leaders. (Resources can become negative if they go outside the control of the leader, e.g. a corrupt family member, or rebellious army.)
- the *cont*ext of their leadership – the things they cannot directly control at a particular moment.

The familiar reasons why leaders may opt for war can be linked to these three parameters.

- *Ability* – the 'minds of leaders' – their strategic capability, leadership skills, charisma, determination, and knowledge from previous involvement in war
- *Resources* – their armies, information systems, industrial strength, political parties, power networks, and shared interests with other leaders
- *Contexts* – public opinion, world trends, natural resources, climate, and economic strength.

The holistic question is how do these *together* affect how leaders use or abuse their power? The parameters are linked by *relationships*, including perception and trust. Followers, in the form of civil society, cannot have much direct impact on 'abilities' or 'resources', but they can create a relational context in which these might change.

Some phenomena can be 'context' or 'resources', according to circumstances, the media for instance. Some aspects are 'transferable context' but some are 'fixed'. A leader may transfer men from 'context' to 'resources' by creating military service, but factors such as the weather are nontransferable. Internet is providing another dimension – the possibility for followers to create their own leaderless 'resources' to challenge and control traditional leadership. The South Korean elections in December 2002 were significantly influenced by home pages of 'netizens', which supported the successful candidate, Roh Moo Hyun, not his pro-US anti-unification opponent Lee Hoi Chang.

One of the main explanations for the demise of aggressive regimes is that their 'resources' become stressed and exhausted, and that 'transferable context' also becomes stressed or not available. The Soviet Union seems the obvious example. Unplanned, this is also the effect that terrorists are having on the US, where intelligence systems are saturated with information, and the military is too stretched to protect Americans overseas. This proposes a strategy for hastening the decline of a despot. Information overload is the main weapon. A dictator, who must utilise his/her 'resources' and 'transferable context' for fighting a major information war, will have little capacity left to utilise them for other means of maintaining power. And this is war without violence.

The lack of academic interest in the relationship between leadership and war means a lack of questioning. When leadership is placed as the unit of analysis, there are very obvious examples to consider. Why is it unthinkable that the Dalai Lama would promote war, or advocate suicide bombing? The circumstances of his people are certainly analogous to those of Palestinians. Religious belief cannot be the only answer. A proper observance of Islam would outlaw suicide bombing in Israel because it leads to the death of women and children. Is it because the Dalai Lama perceives himself as a living god? And as a result, his leadership embraces the whole of humanity, so it is unthinkable that he would advocate the killing any human being. War has already been made unthinkable for particular forms of leadership, yet we have not asked why or how.

2. Unmade in the minds of 'men'

In a world where conflicts and the threat of mass destruction seem omnipresent, it is hard to remember that we are also in a world where there are significant examples of war having been made unthinkable in the minds of leaders. In which contexts has that been achieved and can the principles be extended?

2.1 MAD

The first example is perhaps uncomfortable but must be acknowledged – nuclear deterrence. Whether of not the threat of Mutually Assured Destruction (MAD), makes war more or less thinkable will be probably argued about until the day that the former view is evidenced by a nuclear holocaust. But half a century of the threat of nuclear extinction has passed without it happening. The biographies of those who have had their fingers on the nuclear button disclose very little about how individuals have reconciled their personal conscience with the possibility of having to 'do their duty' as public officials, and perhaps exterminate a large sector of humanity. The nearest we seem to get to a clear answer to the question, 'Would you have pushed the button', has been, 'I did not know that I would not.'[xxxiv]

MAD has not made war unthinkable – arguably the reverse in some contexts. It has seemingly made the use of nuclear weapons less thinkable, but that is a unique circumstance from which it is hard to generalise about other contexts that lessen the likelihood of war. But there is one generalisable aspect. So far, MAD has de-linked war and violence.

The concept of de-linking war from violence may become of greater significance in an increasingly technological world. John Gray concludes that beyond 'the ragged armies of the poor...', '[w]ars are no longer fought by conscript armies but by computers ...'[xxxvi] The idea is reflected in the views of Korean politician Lee- Sang-Hee, who argues that conscription is redundant in the context of future technological warfare. Virtual war creates the possibility that, as suggested above (1.4), wars could soon really be fought between leaders, without significant harm to others. And if countries have smaller armies of technical experts, the military are less likely to be used to maintain authoritarian governments through brute force.

Virtual war also raises another possibility, the full inclusion of women in warfare. The argument is not that women are intrinsically against war, nor about equal opportunities. As has been demonstrated in the workplace and parliament, the inclusion of women in male-dominated settings brings new dynamics and new ideas. In the male domain of war, women may well contribute intellectual tools that can help to de-link war from violence. There are already precedents. The use of Japanese soldiers as part of the peacekeeping forces in East Timor is not only significant because this is the first time since World War Two that Japanese soldiers have been deployed internationally. It is also significant because many of those soldiers were women.

2.2 Regionalisation

The second context – supra-state regionalisation – demands more detailed consideration, because the trend is towards creating regional identities. These aim directly or indirectly to increase security in its broadest sense, and that concept is replicable in many ways. Since 1945, over a hundred such regional agreements have been made.[xxxvii] Historically, we perhaps forget that the minds of leaders have already made war virtually unthinkable within formerly warring regions such as a United Kingdom and a United States of America. Europe is the more familiar example. There are other less obvious instances, which western minds do not appreciate. These include the United States of Mexico, the People's Republic of China, the former Soviet Union and Warsaw Pact countries, Nasser's attempt to create a United Arab Republic, and the recent African Union. Regions not only foster peace internally. They can broker peace elsewhere. Currently, the EU is working unobtrusively with North Korea.[xxxviii]

Although the political impetus to regionalise Europe came directly from the two world (European) wars, the idea was established much earlier. The publication of Kant's *Perpetual Peace a Philosophical Sketch* in 1795 is often seen as the origins of a unified Europe, but arguably the vision of regionalisation can be traced back to the Renaissance and figures such as Juan Luis Vives and Hugo Grotius. The idea is also evident in works such as William Penn's *Present and Future Peace of Europe* (1693), and Jeremy Bentham's *Plan for a Universal and Perpetual Peace* (1786-89).[xxxix] The lesson from history is that an idea must wait for an opportunity before it can become reality, and that may take a long time. But history also reminds us of the corollary, that good ideas eventually find their opportunity. Mike Moore, former Director-General of the WTO, claims of prescient leadership, 'It is wrong to be right too soon'.[xl] The idea of making war unthinkable is perhaps an example.

Regions that are not based on geographical adjacency arguably have had a similar effect to that envisaged for a united Europe – the Commonwealth seems an example, as do trade blocs such as The Association of South East Asian Nations (ASEAN) and the Economic Community of West African States (ECOWAS). It is also relevant to consider regional international governmental organisations (IGOs) such as the Arab League. The OECD and IMF have made Japan economically part of the west, and the possibility of a war between Japan and the west is certainly now unthinkable. The WTO may have similar effect. That is likely to be an underlying reason for admitting China and Taiwan within twenty-four hours of one another, in 2001. With the specific purpose of security, NATO similarly links two geographically distant regions, which we forget have not historically always been at peace. If we view the planet also as a region, the League of Nations and United Nations also become part of the regionalisation and security picture.

The significant point about the modern regions is their federal nature and plurality of power – no single leader has absolute power. Leaders are part of a regional leadership; they are not regional leaders. In contrast, the older regions of China, US, and UK have single overlords. Is it just coincidence that these older regions seem to display a greater propensity for war than the newer ones with a greater plurality of leadership? The newer regions seem to combine two ideas – that a common interest makes war less thinkable, and the (supposedly Confucian) truism that 'Good fences make good neighbours'.

There is another notable aspect of supra-regions. Political parties less often feature as an aspect of a regional leadership's 'resources'. It is arguable that political parties do little to benefit the public in a national setting. They only assist leaders as individuals, and that assistance has often been in relation to war. Hitler and Mussolini would not have got far without the Nazi and Fascist parties. Communist leaders are inherently the product of their political parties. The Catch 22 is that few political leaders will criticise the idea of political parties. And this denial is compounded through the coincidence of interest between political leaders throughout the world, even if adversaries. The party of the opposition can be criticised, but not the concept of parties. Regions usually de-link leaders from political parties, and that seems to make war less thinkable.

De-linking politicians from parties can also be achieved through utilising democratic processes. Civil society organisations might adopt a policy of encouraging people to vote for independent candidates. In parallel, there might be a greater exposure of the dynamics that make political parties a historical legacy that is of questionable value to the general populace, and of the circumstances in which parties have clearly been a precipitant of war. This is not such a dramatic idea. The leaders of multi-national companies are not hampered by having to work within political parties, and many of them now run organisations that have a bigger budget than many countries.

The arms trade, international law and technological vulnerability make modern war intrinsically a regional context for leaders. Many conflicts have shown how weapons can end up being used against their manufacturers and their allies. A leader who permits his/her soldiers to rape women anywhere in the war region, will now be held responsible for that conduct. If a leader permits his/her army to win by causing major environmental damage to achieve victory (e.g. by bombing a nuclear power station or chemicals factory), the job of putting that right may eventually fall to that leader. Environmental impacts do not respect borders, and so problems may well be own goals or have global impacts. It is often claimed that modern democracies have avoided war, but is it that these nations are coincidentally technologically vulnerable, and have too much to lose? The international context of war entails a regional/global interest and responsibility, but that is not widely recognised. If not regional/global leaders, we need regionally/globally-minded leaders.

2.3 *The planetary region*

If the planet were seen as a region, would the development of a pluralist planetary leadership create a world in which war is unthinkable? There are precedents. If we look at leaders within the international organistions, that seems to be true. It is hard to envision Director-Generals such as Gro Harlem Brundtland (WTO), Mary Robinson (UNHCR) or Mike Moore (WTO) as thinking of war is a rational response to any situation, however threatening. Yet these particular international leaders have all been national leaders and, at least technically, that means they would have been prepared to sanction war in their national interests.

But this list is selective. These were all national leaders with a planetary-regional vision of some sort – leaders who recognised a global or 'Planetary Interest'.[xli] Brundtland originated the concept of sustainable development in *Our Common Future (Our Common Future: The World Commission on Environment and Development*, Chair, Gro Harlem Bruntland, New York: Oxford University Press, 1987). Mary Robinson had promoted global human rights for many years. Mike Moore was dedicated to the idea of free world trade well before he headed the WTO. It seems that there is more to the personality of leaders who eschew war than their job title. The key factor is that they have a planetary vision, and that has arisen because of an interaction between their 'ability' and the context in which they found themselves. Brundtland, for example, was a medical doctor and was strongly influenced by her father who was an international medic. She then had the chance, as prime minister of a progressive nation, to promote a vision of sustainable development and later at the WHO, the vision of 'Healthy people – healthy planet'.[xlii] We need to understand better the context in which some leaders perceive themselves as part of a global leadership, even when working at a national level?

One explanation is that some leaders recognise the concept of common threats. International relations classes sometimes engage in counterfactual analysis of the consequences of the threat of invading aliens from another planet. One conclusion is common. National leaders would forget their differences and unify into a planetary leadership, to fight the common foe. The concept of global security – which links environment, development and conflict – tries to build this ethos through presenting the new common 'threats without enemies', such as climate change and ozone depletion, in the form of security discourse.[xliii] Current discussions about the Earth being hit by asteroids are in this genre. Even if this threat is remote, the process of addressing it could engender more global forms of leadership.

2.4 Cosmopolitan

The main progenitor of a planetary region is probably not global politics, but the increase in population movement throughout the world – greater cosmopolitanism through international living[xliv] and transnational communities.[xlv] The British population comprises three hundred and forty spoken languages and thirty-three national groups of more than ten thousand people. By 2001, the number of immigrants became more than the natural growth of the population. The increase in international living may not guarantee peace, but it constructs a context in which too many people have too much to lose from war, and leaders are likely to recognise that.

The idea of reducing the propensity for war through uniting Europe can be traced back even earlier than prescient texts, and interestingly to leadership and elites. Arranged marriages within elite European families were intended to reduce conflict and increase trade. The marriage between King Henry VIII and Catherine of Aragon, aimed to link England with Spain and the Hapsburg Empire. Similar arrangements occurred in other parts of the word, for example in East Asia, and were accompanied by a near acceptance of mistresses and concubines signalling that these arranged marriages were for the purpose of international not human relations. The Jordanian Royal family provides a notable contemporary example of marriages that, although not arranged, have contributed to international harmony and regional security.

International marriage is not now just the privilege of a few elites, and this aspect of globalisation clearly reduces the likelihood of popular support for war. Most countries have a significant number of nationals with family links in other nations. In Germany one in six families is transnational. Even in hitherto homogenous Japan, the proportion of marriages to someone from outside Japan is now one in thirty-five. Interestingly, international marriage also brings the same benefits to communities that were achieved through the appropriation of women as a prize of primitive warfare – genetic diversity and an exchange of ideas and culture (see above 1.1).

The role of leadership is not now to arrange unpalatable marriages between themselves, or even to promote international marriage between their followers. It is to reduce the barriers to international marriage for everyone. So far they have failed to achieve this, and have actively blocked this simple and cheap route to enhancing international relations and security. In the UK, a 'spouse visa' for legal married immigrants takes up to three years to obtain. Japan can issue the same visa in three days.

3. Changing the minds of 'men'

Regions create 'contexts' and 'resources' in which war becomes less thinkable. Potentially warring factions are constrained by the institutions, systems, cross-border economic interests, codes and ethos, and cosmopolitan communities. And the reduced influence from political parties removes a major progenitor of war. But might a 'personal resource' – the mind of a leader – be changed because of these dynamics? Regionally- minded leaders, even if nationally based, seem less inclined to war. The world certainly seemed safer with a globally-minded Clinton as president of the US, than with a provincially-minded George Bush.

3.1 Self-perception

The basic self-perception mechanisms seem simple. If regional leaders proposed war, they would be proposing war against themselves, because they are responsible for a regional interest. War framed in this manner is not a rational act, and leaders do not want to perceive themselves as irrational, so war is avoided. Similarly, the ethic that binds regional leaderships together is about group and territorial unity, and it would be contradictory to create group divisions as is common among leaders who want to create war (1.3). Again, no leader wants to appear self-contradictory.

Self-perception theory supports the idea that contexts are important. D.J. Bem's original premise is that people come to know their internal states 'partially by inferring them from observations of their own behaviour and/or the circumstances in which this behaviour occurs.'[xlvi] For example, politicians who observe themselves enthusiastically applauding a particular speech may infer that this is because they agree with that speech and are therefore ideologically a member of that political group. But 'circumstances' also play a part. Those who find themselves spontaneously applauding an unknown speaker, will perceive this as greater agreement than if they are routinely applauding a colleague who they know they wish to please. When there are no obvious alternative circumstantial explanations for particular behaviour, self-perception mechanisms will be strongest and will draw conclusions from self-observation. Leaders who observe themselves in the context of a regional leadership seem more likely to perceive themselves as having regional responsibility, and this perception is strong because there are few alternative explanations.

The significance of self-perception theory is that it sets up 'the conditions for attitude change ... if attitudes are determined by behaviour rather than the other way around, then modification of behaviour will produce concomitant modification of attitude.'[xlvii] It seems possible to change the minds of leaders through creating a 'context' in which they perceive themselves as having regional responsibility, even if they are not regional leaders. But how can this be done?

3.2 Persona

In the classical Roman theatre, persona was the mask that an actor wore to express the role being played. Jung then used the term to mean the role a person takes on because of social pressures – a role that society expects someone to play – the public face. Are there social pressures, perhaps brought about by civil society, which can change a leader's *persona*, from provincial to regional?

One approach is to return to the significance of 'relational context' (1.5), and employ a theoretical framework developed by Lee, who proposes that the relations, including perceptions, can be viewed in two categories: 'hard' relations, which are coercive, law-based and rooted in written codes. And 'soft' relations which are negotiated, empathy-based and reflect social norms and traditions (In Korea, the concepts 'soft' and 'hard' are understood in terms of Korean culture, but are expressed in English.) The relations of a coercive politician such as Korea's President Park exemplifies the former, and public empathy with the personal experiences of a leader such as Nelson Mandela reflects the latter.[xlviii] Most leaders are likely to use, and be perceived to use, a mixture of both 'soft' and 'hard' – carrot-and-stick – relations (The same phrase is used in Korean – *chea zik* [whip] – *dang gun* [carrot]). The effectiveness probably arises because of the link between the two. Like the donkey, followers do not have a clear perception of what is leading them, and so challenge, and refusal, becomes less easy. But leaders can also be led by followers, through the effective linking of 'hard' and 'soft' relations.

3.2.1. 'Hard' relations

Precipitating *persona* changes in relation to 'hard' relationships is probably easiest to envisage. These would come about through reference to the frameworks now provided by international law, other codes of conduct, or emergent norms such as the global/planetary interest[xlix] and enforcement institutions such as the Yugoslav and Arusha war tribunals. National courts also have a role. In December 2002, CND started a case in the high court against the UK government on the basis that a war with Iraq would be unlawful without UN consent. This was the first case of its kind.[1] Leaders intrinsically wish to appear strong. So the strategy is to propose the need for strong leadership to uphold a regional interest and international norms. Leaders who follow popularist calls for aggression or act out of self-interest, should be seen as weak.

Although the centrality of leadership to world security is readily accepted, there is no formal international code of

conduct regulating global leadership.[li] Formally acknowledging the responsibility of identifiable leaders within
codes that restrain aggression and violence, would probably greatly improve their effectiveness.[lii] The Chemical
Weapons Convention provides a rare example. This
requires registration of the name of the owner of factories
that can produce chemicals that could be utilised in
weapons.[liii] But the lack of codification of leadership
responsibility is perhaps not so surprising. The minds of
leaders also control whether or not they regulate themselves.

3.2.2. 'Soft' relations

'Soft' change is more subtle, and stems from a psychological truism that we are all 'a reaction to the reaction to us'.
The reaction of others to our *persona* will create a reaction
by us, which then evolves the *persona* we use in the future.

Simple experiments show that daily interaction is related to our outward appearance. For example, a young
attractive woman asking busy bus conductors foolish
questions will get helpful accommodating answers. But if
the same woman is dressed and made-up as an older
woman, she acts as if having a mental disability, and she
asks the same foolish questions, the response is usually
less helpful and sometimes hostile. As a reaction to this,
people who actually have this experience may take on the
persona of an aggressive individual, and they get caught in
a negative '*persona* trap'.

Other lessons about marginalised people can be applied
to powerful leaders. Professionals who work with people
with mental disabilities who display 'challenging behaviour' (aggression or violence) employ straightforward psychology: they ignore bad behaviour and reward good,
unless there is an immediate likelihood of harm. To
acknowledge bad behaviour, even in the form of punishment, can become a reward. For people with mental

disabilities and powerful leaders alike, the reward of gaining attention can outweigh the pain of punishment. Rewards are often symbolic – maybe just simple praise. For leaders, symbolic rewards such as Peace Prizes, de-link the evolutionary/biological demand for the rewards of aggression, from rewards that have real value, such as water and land.

Punishment is avoided because it will be seen as unjust or irrelevant, and may precipitate aggression. If remedial action is necessary, it is decided outside the heat of an irritating event. If critical comment is necessary, then the rule is 'condemn the behaviour not the person'. Academics who have studied people responsible for torture point out that men who can order or carry out horrible atrocities, may at home be wonderful, gentle loving husbands and fathers. It is therefore more accurate to talk of, 'People who torture' rather than, 'Torturers'. Condemning the action and not the person leaves the possibility for rehabilitation.

Like marginalised people, marginalised leaders may need facilitation to take part in discussions and negotiations. Facilitation is considered necessary in relation to minority groups, but it is hard to extend this ethos to people who we have been taught to hate. We need to extend contemporary principles of redressing social exclusion to apparent despots. They need to be drawn into the international community, not pushed away. Exclusion, whether in a psychiatric hospital or a palace, is not going to create people who can contribute to the building of a safer world, because this does not build the empathy necessary for 'soft' relations in a large community.

Is it possible to engender regional and global *personas* and changes in self-perception through the media? Would a CNN programme that showed Saddam Hussein positively as part of a global leadership help to change his perception of himself or lessen the (supposed) threat he poses? Would a portrayal of Israeli leaders as part of a regional Middle East leadership have a similar effect? At present, the media usually presents a stereotypical view of these leaders as isolationist. Other forms of information technology might be employed. Isolationist leaders could take part in public videoconference meetings of international leaders – virtual G-meetings.

3.2.3 Carrot-and-stick

A carrot-and stick approach links 'hard' and 'soft' relations. The building of relational contexts that engender a positive persona and self-perception change therefore includes

'Hard'
- International codes and other norms that constrain aggression and violence
- Codes that put specific responsibilities on identifiable leaders
- A public view that strong leaders support these norms, and weak leaders do not.

'Soft'
- A realisation that even powerful people become 'a reaction to the reaction to them'
- A greater responsibility within the international community, and civil society, to break negative 'persona traps'
- Condemning poor personal conduct, not the person
- Rewarding good conduct, and (if safe to do so) ignoring bad
- Utilising symbolic rewards linked to status
- Facilitating and supporting apparent despots to take part in negotiations
- Presenting excluded provincial leaders in a global or regional context, through the media and IT

As with good horse-riding, the ultimate goal of using a carrot-and-stick approach is that the stick is effective because it is there, not because it is used. Like the whip of a good horse-rider or the sword of a modern king, enforcement measures should become largely symbolic.

4. Changing minds in Korea

The Korean peninsula provides an instance of an ongoing 'international war'(Other examples of international conflict, such as Kashmir or Cyprus, are not framed in terms of a declared war.). North Korean President Kim Jong Il is presented as an international recluse who is a threat to world security. He is also presented as a leader who harms his own people through oppressive social control,[liv] appropriation of resources and consequent mass poverty, and through imprisoning his opposition in labour camps[lv] where pregnant women are forced to have abortions or their infants are killed.[lvi] Such stories are presented by western observers, and usually at times when it thought necessary to construct Kim Jong Il as an enemy leader. Whatever the truth, North Korea seems to show that provincially-minded leaders are more inclined to war, and the peninsular exemplifies other important themes.

Korea demonstrates that paradoxical coincidences of interests between leaders can fuel war. In November 2002, the *Herald Tribune* reported an exchange of military technology between North Korea and Pakistan. North Korea had allegedly supplied Pakistan with ballistic missile parts, and Pakistan had provided North Korea with machinery to improve its production of highly enriched uranium. The Pakistani plane that took the missile parts from North Korea to Pakistan was a Lockheed-built C-130, made available to Pakistan by the US leadership, in return for Pakistan's cooperation in the US 'War against terrorism'.[lvii] A few days later, a ship carrying scud missiles from North Korea to Yemen was intercepted, but it was permitted to continue because the US did not want to upset Yemen when a war with Iraq seemed immanent.[lviii] War is now intrinsically regional/global.

In September 2002, *The People's Korea* website provided 'answers to written questions raised by the president of the Kyodo News Service', by Kim Jong Il, which included the following statement

> Korea and Japan are geographically close countries, and they had maintained relations from olden times exchanging visits with each other. But in the past century discord and confrontation have brought the relations between the two countries to an extremely abnormal state ... Normalizing relations between the two countries and developing good-neighborly relations accords with the aspirations and interests of the peoples of the two countries ...
>
> Korea and Japan are Asian nations. They should live in friendship as nearest neighbours, not as near yet distant neighbors, and promote coexistence and co-prosperity. This is our will and consistent standpoint.[lix]

The significance is not just about relations with Japan, which is probably due to North Korea's economic problems. It is that Kim Jong Il chose to adopt a regional argument, yet he seems an unlikely advocate of regional concern. Did the planned meeting with Japan's prime minister Koizumi four days later engender in Kim a *persona* of being a regional leader because he was treated as a regional leader? Did he perceive himself as a regional leader, because he observed himself as part of a regional leadership, as self-perception theory proposes (3.1)?

Whatever the truth, why did the international community not react to this statement? World leaders might have encouraged Kim's newfound regional concern through

promoting Korean unification and encouraging international dialogue. Current international rhetoric is about
controlling weapons of mass destruction in the North, not
about full reunification of Korea, as in Germany. Why? It is
very probable that a unified Korea would quickly become
a significant economic rival for Japan, the US, Russia,
China and Europe. So there is a disincentive for national
leaders outside Korea to encourage full unification, but
also within the peninsula, because this would reduce the
power of most Korean leaders. This dynamic was demonstrated by the campaign by the South Korean opposition
party, the Grand National Party (GNP), against the unification minister Lim Dong-Won, in 2001. The GNP accused
Lim of a technical breach of the law, which prohibits prais-
ing the North. Constructive dialogue is hard if the minister
cannot display a few courtesies towards the North. The
persona of an aggressive leader is being constructed, and
war fuelled, through coincidences of leadership interests,
internal and external.

Acceptance that Korea may not be fully unified may
seem strange to outsiders. But this policy may create
another pluralist region, not much different from the
United Kingdom, and only differing from the EU in scale
and complexity. Historically, Korea was three nations from
the fourth to seventh century, and two from 698-926 AD.
Perhaps ultimately a regional pluralist Korean leadership
will bring greater stability than would a fully unified
Korea.

Since July 1953, the Korean War has been a war without
significant violence. Has South Korea's lead in economic
and technological development extended, unnoticed, to
demonstrating a lead in how we unthink war, through de-
linking war and violence? The demise of oppressive leadership in the North is likely to come about because the
'resources' of the regime become exhausted and the world
'context' no longer provides the needed 'transferable

resources' (1.5). The international community could probably hasten this process, if it wanted to.

At the Asian games in Busan in September 2002, athletes from North and South Korea entered the stadium holding hands. They also carried a flag showing the whole Korean peninsula as blue, as did the teams at the Inter-Korean football match.[ix] It is unlikely that this would have happened without agreement from power elites in North and South. Create the right context and leaders recognise that the evolutionary/biological drivers of war can be de-linked from war, and they even use the context to promote peace. In sports, the competing is real but the prize is symbolic – a medal. Leaders attending the games observed themselves as part of a regional leadership, and their self-perception may change accordingly.

Accompanying the North Korean athletes were many conspicuously beautiful young North Korean women. Local men were so impressed that a North Korean dialect became fashionable in Busan. More surprisingly, the clothes and hairstyles of the North Korean women reflected current western fashions. Again, this is likely to have been sanctioned from the highest level. Was this another signal that Kim Jong Il was starting to think globally? Kim is known to pay attention to such details. In 1996, he took personal responsibility for redesigning the uniforms of his own traffic police, who also 'appear to be chosen for their beauty'.[lxi] If intelligence agencies employed more women, perhaps the significance of such details would be noticed and built upon.

In the right context, the prey of male warfare can become the leaders who show that evolutionary/biological drivers can operate in different ways. Historically, if not a prize of war, women have often cheered and encouraged their men to go and fight. Can they now show second-track global leadership and support men who want to find alternatives to war? In May 2002, Ms Park Keun Hye, daughter of the former president Park Chung Hee, went to the North to meet Kim Jong Il and the *National Reconciliation Council*.[lxii] Then in October, women students from North and South gathered at Mt. Kumgang, as did Korean women overseas, to promote reconciliation and cooperation.[lxiii] The world media ignored both events. The role of Korean women in peacemaking is not new. In 1919, during Japanese occupation, Yu Gwan Sun was among activists who organised a peaceful protest in the form of a 'Declaration of Independence' distributed to thirty-five thousand Christian, Buddhist and other Korean leaders, in three days. She was imprisoned, where she died.

The refusal to give Kim Jong Il the Nobel Peace Prize, when it is was given to Kim Dae Jung following the historic handshake between the two Kims, is a major failure of the international community. It would have rewarded good behaviour while ignoring bad, and engendered 'soft' empathy, but in relation to 'hard' traditional norms of the prize. It would have helped to build Kim Jong Il's international *persona*, probably evolved his self-perception and reversed his provincialism and international exclusion. It might have started to de-link him from his Korean People's Party. His status would have been enhanced, and he would have captured a major symbolic possession, with no violence. All this for the cost of a medal. There is more to be gained from using a Peace Prize to reward the good behaviour of a 'bad leader', than from giving it to a saint.

5. Conclusion: re-linking the minds of 'men'

Leaders invent war by linking and de-linking functions, circumstances and ideas – and naming events and concepts – to suit their own purposes. So, re-linking – alternative linking and de-linking – may help to make war less thinkable. A framework can be constructed in relation to the three parameters of leadership. Linking and de-linking are a matter of degree, and do not imply total unity or separation. Many of the strategies are, of course, not new. But it is the possibility of a holistic approach, within civil society and its 'netizens', which presents the likelihood of greater efficacy.

This re-linking builds a bigger idea – de-linking war from violence. The phrase appears an oxymoron, yet history provides many examples. Put another way, 'wars' involve force but need not use violence. Gandhi, like Yu Gwan Sun, used non-violent force, and his 'war' tactics avoided directly attacking the British army. The British forces did not build group solidarity in the way that armies usually do because of attack. Perhaps British leaders eventually sensed this, and so sought a resolution. Contrast this with armies that have presented themselves as invincible and willing to use any degree of violence to win – the Japanese in World War Two, and Hitler against the Russians. The result was eventual defeat. The lesson from history, which seems to have been well-disguised for too long, is that one way to win a war is by not using violence. This is especially relevant to modern asymmetrical war, which cannot be won by force, only by removing the motivation of the aggressors. In future war, the leader who avoids harming the opposing force is more likely to win, and the tools of information and computing technology make this more thinkable.

War is made by leaders, but so are peace and security, and many other 'goods' of life. Without leaders we would not have war, but without leaders we would probably still exist in the primitive context of petty feuding for the purpose of men obtaining women and other instinct-based rewards. Historically, it is progressive leaders – intellectual, religious, political – who have shown us that this is an undesirable state, and have created the social systems to bring about change. It is leaders who can make war unthinkable by de-linking war from violence. The message to them is that this is one of two scenarios in which war becomes unthinkable. The other is a world in which no one follows leaders. Information technology is making that a possibility, but perhaps that is not a scenario that will lead us to a better world overall.

References

[i] Buchanan, Mark, *Ubiquity* (London: Weidenfeld & Nicolson, 2000) p. 190

[ii] Rubin, Barry, 'The real roots of Arab anti-Americanism', in *Foreign Affairs*, November/December 2002, pp. 73-85

[iii] Mackenzie, D. and M. le Page, 'Act now' plea on bioterror threat, *New Scientist*, 28 September 2002, p. 4

[iv] Gray, John (2002) *Straw dogs: thoughts on humans and other animals* (London: Granta Books, 2002) p.182

[v] Fromm, Erich, *The Anatomy of Human Destructiveness* (London: Penguin, 1973)

[vi] Pinker, Steven, *How the mind works* (London: Allen Lane, 1997) 509.

[vii] Turnbull, Colin M., *Man in Africa* (Harmondsworth: Penguin, 1976), p. 83.

[viii] Mead, M., 'Warfare is only an invention – not a biological necessity', in *Asia*, 40, no 8 (1940) pp. 402-5

[ix] Wright, Q., *A study of war* (Chicago: University of Chicago Press: Chicago, 1965)

[x] Fromm, Erich, *The anatomy of human destructiveness* (London: Penguin, 1973) pp. 279, 289, 290

[xi] Williams, Christopher, *Leaders of integrity: ethics and a code for global leadership* (Amman: United Nations University Leadership Academy, 2001), p. 72

[xii] Williams, Christopher (2001) *Leaders of integrity: ethics and a code for global leadership* (Amman: United Nations University Leadership Academy, 2001) pp. 65-74.

[xiii] Fromm, Erich, *The anatomy of human destructiveness* (London: Penguin, 1973), p. 288

[xiv] Thompson, Mark, *Forging war: the media in Serbia, Croatia, Bosnia, and Hercegovina* (Luton: University of Luton Press, 2000), pv

[xv] Mazower, Mark, *The Balkans* (London: Weidenfeld & Nicolson, 2000), p. 129

[xvi] Berkeley, Bill, *The graves are not yet full: race, tribe, and power in the heart of Africa* (New York: Basic Books, 2001), p.14

[xvii] Rubin, Barry, 'The real roots of Arab anti-Americanism', in *Foreign Affairs*, November/December 2002, pp. 79,80

[xviii] Berkeley, Bill, *The graves are not yet full: race, tribe, and power in the heart of Africa* (New York: Basic Books, 2001), p. 120

[xix] Herzog, Roman, *Preventing the clash of civilizations: a peace strategy for the twenty-first century* (New York: St Martins Press, 1999)

[xx] Gray, John, *Straw dogs: thought on humans and other animals* (London: Granta Books, 2002) p.181

[xxi] See: Zubok, Vladislav M., CPSU *Plenums, leadership struggles, and Soviet Cold War politics* (Cold War International History Project) Woodrow Wilson International Centre for Scholars, CWIHP Document (2002).

[xxii] Norton-Taylor, Richard and Owen Bowcott, 'Deadly cost of the new warfare', in *The Guardian*, 22 October 1999, p. 3.

[xxiii] Fromm, Erich, *The anatomy of human destructiveness* (London: Penguin, 1973) p. 288.

[xxiv] Fisk, Robert, 'He is alive...' *The Independent*, 14 November 2002, p. 3.

[xxv] Fromm, Erich, *The anatomy of human destructiveness* (London: Penguin, 1973) London, p. 286

[xxvi] Fisk, Robert, With runners and whispers, al-Qa'ida outfoxes US forces, *The Independent*, 6 December 2002, p. 15.

[xxvii] Nussbaum, A., *A concise history of the law of nations* (New York: Macmillan, 1962), p. 4.

[xxviii] Morgenthau, Hans J., *Politics among nations: the struggle for power and peace* (New York: Alfred A Knopf, 1963)

[xxix] Turnbull, Colin M., *Man in Africa* (Harmondsworth: Penguin, 1976), pp. 82, 31.

[xxx] Peake, Gordon, *War Lords and Peace Lords: political leadership in conflicted societies*, www.incore.ulst.ac.uk/home/research/pngoing/wlpl.html

[xxxi] Vasquez, John A. et al (eds.), *Beyond Confrontation: learning conflict resolution in the Post-Cold War era* (Ann Arbor: Univ. of Michigan Press, 1995)

[xxxii] Fromm, Erich, *The anatomy of human destructiveness* (London: Penguin, 1973)

[xxxiii] Lee, Yun Joo, Perceptions of leadership and development in South Korea and Egypt, unpublished PhD thesis in progress, SOAS, University of London, Chapter 3 (2002)

[xxxiv] See similar in: Barker, C. and A. Johnson, *Leadership and social movements* (Manchester: Manchester University Press, 2001)

[xxxv] Answer by the commander of a nuclear submarine, to the author

[xxxvi] Gray, John, *Straw dogs: thoughts on humans and other animals* (London: Granta Books, 2002), p. 162

[xxxvii] Scholte, Jan Aart, 'The globalisation of world politics', in J. Baylis and S. Smith, *The globalistion of world politics: and introduction to international relations* (Oxford: Oxford University Press, 2001), p. 24

[xxxviii] The People's Korea (2002) Park Chung Hee's daughter goes to North; Kim Jong Il meets Ms Park, www.korea-np.co.jp/pk/180th_issue/2002052501.htm

[xxxix] D'Appollonia, Ariane Chebel, 'European Nationalism and European Union', in Anthony Pagden, *The Idea of Europe: from antiquity to the European Union* (Cambridge: Cambridge University Press, 2002), pp.171-190

[xl] Moore, Mike, *A brief history of the future: citizenship of the Millennium* (Christchurch: Shoal Bay Press, 1998)

[xli] Graham, Kennedy, *The planetary interest* (London: UCL Press, 1999)

[xlii] Graham, K. and C. Williams (eds.), *Healthy people – healthy planet: an interview with Gro Harlem Brundtland, Director-*

General of the WHO (Amman: United Nations University Leadership Academy, 2002)

[xliii] Prins, Gwyn, *Threats without enemies: facing environmental insecurit*, (London: Earthscan, 1993)

[xliv] Wallace, John A., *The experiment in International Living: a brief history of its international development* 1932-1992. (London: Alan C. Hood & Co., 1996)

[xlv] Portes, Alejandro (1997) *Globalisation from below: the rise of transnational communities*, http://www.transcomm.ox.ac.uk/working%20papers/portes.pdf

[xlvi] Bem, D.J., Self-perception theory, in L. Berkowitz (ed.), *Advances in experimental social psychology*, Vol. 6 (New York: Academic Press, 1972), p. 5.

[xlvii] Reber, Arthur S., *Dictionary of psychology* (London: Penguin, 1995), p. 703

[xlviii] Lee, Yun Joo, 'Perceptions of leadership and development in South Korea and Egypt'. Unpublished PhD in progress. University of London, SOAS (2002)

[xlvix] Graham, Kennedy, *The planetary interest* (London: UCL Press, 1999)

[l] Pallister, D., 'CND asks court to tie attack to new UN resolution', *The Guardian*, 10 December 2002, p. 13

[li] Williams, Christopher, *Leaders of integrity: ethics and a code for global leadership* (Amman: United Nations University Leadership Academy, 2001)

[lii] Williams, Christopher, *Leaders of integrity: ethics and a code for global leadership* (Amman: United Nations University Leadership Academy, 2001), pp. 65-69

[liii] Chemical Weapons Convention Part vii, 6(a), 7(a), 10(a)

[liv] Oh, Kongdan and R.C. Hassig, *North Korea through the looking glas*, (Washington: Brookings Institute, 2000)

[lv] Larkin, John, 'North Korea's secret slave camps are finally exposed to view', *The Independent*, 6 December 2002, p. 16

[lvi] Brooke, James, 'In prisons, swift death for babies', *The Independent*, 12 May 2002, p. 15

[lvii] Sanger, David E., 'Atomic ties link North Korea and Pakistan', in *International Herald Tribune*, 25 November 2002, p. 1

[lviii] Cornwell, Rupert, 'How a show of force in the war on terror turned into an explosive farce', *The Independent*, 12 December 2002, p. 1

[lvix] The People's Korea, Kim Jong Il answers questions raised by Japanese Kyodo News Service, 14 September 2002, www.korea-np.co.jp/pk/183rd_issue/200209/01.mtm

[lx] The People's Korea (2002), North and South Korea unite as one in inter-Korean soccer match, www.korea-np.co.jp/pk/184th_issue/2002092810.htm

[lxi] Oh, Kongdan and R.C. Hassig, *North Korea through the looking glas*, (Washington: Brookings Institute, 2000), p. 99

[lxii] The People's Korea (2002), Park Chung Hee's daughter goes to North; Kim Jong Il meets Ms Park, www.korea-np.co.jp/pk/180th_issue/2002052501.htm

[lxiii] The People's Korea (2002), Women and students hold inter-Korean civic rallies, www.kore-np.co.jp/pk/180th_issue/200205052501.htm

APPENDIX ONE

CONTRIBUTORS

Dame Margaret Anstee, former UN Under Secretary-General

General Sir Hugh Beach, former Master General of the Ordinance

Sir Samuel Brittan, former editor of the *Financial Times*

Professor John Cairns Junior, State University, Blacksburg, Virginia USA

Professor Stephen Castles, Director, Queen Elizabeth House, Oxford

Professor Lynn Davies, University of Birmingham

Dr Scilla Elworthy, founder Oxford Research Group and Peace Direct

Judge Richard Goldstone, former Chief Prosecutor UN International Tribunals

Dr Paul Grossrieder, former Director General of the International Committee of the Red Cross

Professor Beatrice Heuser, Director of Research MGFA (Military History Research Office of the Bundeswehr), Potsdam

Professor Robert Hinde, former Master of St John's College, Cambridge

Professor Sir Michael Howard, All Souls, Oxford

Yun-Joo Lee, University of London

Professor Paul Rogers, School of Peace Studies, Bradford University

Professor Sir Joseph Rotblat, physicist, winner Nobel Peace Prize 1995

Imam Dr Abdul Jalil Sajid, Muslim Council of Britain

Dr Javier Solana, Secretary-General of the Council of the European Union, High Representative for the Common Foreign and Security Policy

Professor Frances Stewart, Somerville College, Oxford, Director of CRISE

Professor Hew Strachan, All Souls College, Oxford

Dr M.S. Swaminathan, Chairman of Pugwash

Sir Crispin Tickell, former UK Ambassador to the United Nations

Professor Martin van Creveld, Hebrew University, Jerusalem

Brian W. Walker, former Director General of Oxfam

Professor Paul Wilkinson, University of St Andrews

Dr Chris Williams, Birmingham University, formerly UNULA Jordan

The views of the contributors are their own and not necessarily those of *Preparing for Peace*. All papers may be found on: www.preparingforpeace.org

APPENDIX TWO

ABOUT THE QUAKERS

Quakers respect the creative power of God in every human being and in the world around us. We work through quiet processes for a world where peaceful means bring about just settlements.

Quaker Faith

Quaker faith springs from the experience that each one of us can have a direct relationship with the Divine. Quakers find that by meeting together for communal worship we are empowered to find peace and strength for work in the world.

'Quakers' or 'Friends'

Formally Quakers are the Religious Society of Friends and hence often refer to each other as "Friends". The public more commonly refer to them as Quakers. More than twenty seven thousand people attend Quaker meetings for worship in the UK and Ireland. These quiet times of seeking the presence of God are held in about five hundred places, many of them Quaker-owned Friends' Meeting Houses.

Quaker Witness

Since our foundation in the 1600s in England, Quakers have tried to make a practical witness to our religious convictions. Quakers are especially active in peace work, human rights and social reform.

Quakers Worldwide

Friends World Committee for Consultation (FWCC) was set up at the 1937 World Conference of Friends in Swarthmore, Pennsylvania, USA, 'to act in a consultative capacity to promote better understanding among Friends the world over, particularly by the encouragement of joint conferences and inter-visitation, the collection and circulation of information about Quaker literature and other activities directed towards that end.'

About sixty Yearly Meetings and groups, representing more than three hundred thousand Friends, are affiliated with the FWCC. (Yearly Meeting is the term for a national or sub-continental grouping of Quakers)

Quaker Origins

The movement was founded in England, by George Fox (1624-1691), a nonconformist religious reformer. At the age of 19, he left home on a four year search, seeking answers to questions which had troubled him since his childhood. He sought guidance from a variety of the country's spiritual leaders. He gradually became disillusioned with those leaders and with the existing Christian denominations. At the age of twenty-three, he heard a voice, saying *'there is one, even Christ Jesus, who can speak to thy condition'*. He felt a direct call from God to become an itinerant preacher and promote the concept of the Inward Light, or Inner Voice. He believed that an element of God's spirit is implanted within every person's soul. He called this 'the seed of Christ', or 'the seed of Light'. Thus, everyone has an innate inner capacity to comprehend the word of God and express opinions on spiritual matters.

MEMBERS OF THE PREPARING FOR PEACE PLANNING GROUP

Dr Joseph Hill is a former surgeon and public health specialist at the United Nations. Due to competing demands on his time he stood down from the group at the end of 2003.

Rachel Rogers is co-clerk of Westmorland General Meeting and a founder member of the *Preparing for Peace* project. She is a trustee of the Quaker Tapestry and a former head of Counselling at Lancaster University. She has a lively extended family.

Daphne Sanders is co-clerk of Westmorland General Meeting. Her last job was as an Assistant Director of Social Services. Currently she divides her time between social care, arboriculture and learning Russian.

Dr Eleanor Straughton is currently a research associate at Lancaster University, with a background in history and the social and political sciences.

Brian W. Walker was Director-General of Oxfam for ten years and subsequently President of IIED. (International Institute for Environment and Development).

RECOMMENDED FURTHER READING

Anstee, Margaret Joan, *Never Learn to Type – a Woman at the United Nations* (John Wiley & Sons, 2003)

Bacevich, Andrew J., *The New American Militarism* (OUP 2005)

Beevor, Antony, *Stalingrad* (Penguin, 1998)

Burbach, Roger and Jim Tarbell, *Imperial Overstretch* (Zed Books, 2004)

Chomsky, Noam, *America's Quest for Global Domination* (Penguin, 2002)

Cohen, Stanley, *States of Denial* (Polity, 2001)

Cullinan, Cormac, *Wild Law: A Manifesto for Earth Justice* (Green Books, 2003)

Ferguson, Niall, *The Pity of War* (The Penguin Press, 1998)

Fisher, Simon, Spirited Living (Quaker Books, 2004)

Francis, Diana, *Rethinking War and Peace* (Pluto Press, 2004)

Garton Ash, Timothy, *Free World: why a Crisis of the West Reveals the Opportunity of our Time* (Penguin, 2004)

Hinde, Robert and Joseph Rotblat, *War No More: Eliminating Conflict in the Nuclear Age* (Pluto Press, 2003)

Matthews, Dylan, *War prevention works: 50 stories of people resolving conflict* (Oxford Research Group, 2001)

McNamara, Robert, *In Retrospect* (Random House Times Books, 1995)

Monbiot, George, T*he Age of Consent: a manifesto for a new world order* (Flamingo, 2003)

Owen, Wilfred, *War Poems* (Chatto & Windus, 1994)

Polman, Linda, *We Did Nothing* (Penguin, 1997)

Robertson, Geoffrey, *Crimes Against Humanity* (The Penguin Press, 1999)

Rogers, Paul, *Losing Control: Global Security in the Twenty-first Century* (Pluto, 2000)

Rifkin, Jeremy, *The European Dream: How Europe's Vision of the Future is Quietly Eclipsing the American Dream* (Polity Press, 2004)

Schell, Jonathan, *The Unconquerable World: Power, Nonviolence and the Will of the People* (Allen Lane, 2004)

Stiglitz, Joseph, *Globalization and its discontents* (Penguin, 2002)

Strachan, Hew, *The First World War* (Simon & Schuster, 2003)

Wink, Walter, *The Powers That Be* (Galilee Doubleday, 1998)

NOTES AND REFERENCES

Preface

[1] See Quaker Faith and Practice (1995), Chapter 24: Our Peace Testimony. George Fox, a founder of the Religious Society of Friends (Quakers), stated that in 1651, 'I told [the Commonwealth Commissioners] I lived in the virtue of that life and power that took away the occasion of all wars ... I told them I was come into the covenant of peace which was before wars and strife were', (QFP, 24.01). In perhaps the best known statement of their position, early Friends declared in 1660 that, 'Our principle is, and our practices have always been, to seek peace, and ensure it, and to follow after righteousness and the knowledge of God, seeking the good and welfare, and doing that which tends to the peace of all. All bloody principles and practices we do utterly deny, with all outward wars, and strife, and fightings with outward weapons, for any end, or under any pretence whatsoever, and this is our testimony to the whole world' (QFP, 24.04). Friends' 'peace testimony' is not a written creed or doctrine but rather an evolving body of shared experience, continuing from the seventeenth century to present times.

[2] J. Rotblat (2001), 'The Quest for Global Peace', www.preparingforpeace.org.

Introduction

[3] See B. Walker (2002), Thomas Paine, the Quakers and the Abolition of War, pamphlet, (www.preparingforpeace.org).

[4] We are not alone in rejecting biological determinism as a root cause of war. In 1989, UNESCO endorsed the Seville Statement on Violence in which a world conference of scientists – including neuro-scientists, biologists, social scientists and psychologists – expressed their objection to the idea that human beings are biologically predisposed towards war and violence.

[5] Hinde (2005), 'Why are people willing to go to war?', this volume, p. 72.

[6] See for example the work of the Worldwide Consultative Association of Retired Generals and Admirals (WCARGA), founded in 1993 with the aim of fostering cooperative solutions to crises and preventing armed conflict. WCARGA grew out of the pioneering work of the late Brigadier General Michael Harbottle (previously Chief of Staff of the UN Peacekeeping force in Cyprus) and the movement he helped found as an antidote to the brinkmanship of the Cold War era (Generals for Peace and Disarmament). WCARGA has members in some twenty-five countries around the world.

Part One: Is war a rational tool of politics?

[7] Walker (2003), 'A Quaker's View of Twenty-first Century War', www.preparingforpeace.org.

[8] H. Strachan (2002), 'Can war be controlled and contained?', www.preparingforpeace.org.

[9] We refer here to the Christian Just War principles cited by Hugh Beach in his paper, H. Beach (2005), 'Is war successful in achieving its objectives?', this volume, pp. 107. Beach uses as his source a statement made in 1993 by the United States Catholic Conference, entitled 'The Harvest of Justice is Sown in Peace'

[10] S. Elworthy, (2001), 'How wars could be prevented: Friends' contribution to policy change', www.preparingforpeace.org.

[11] See B. Heuser, 'Is war successful in achieving its objects?', www.preparingforpeace.org.

[12] Walker (2003).

[13] J. Cairns Jnr (2003), 'War and Sustainability', www.preparingforpeace.org. This paper was first published in the *International Journal of Sustainable Development and World Ecology* and is reproduced on our website by kind permission of editor Professor John Jeffers and the Parthenon Publishing Company.

[14] Strachan (2002).

[15] P. Wilkinson (2002), 'Terrorism: Implications for World Peace', www.preparingforpeace.org.

[16] Beach (2005), p. 116.

[17] C. Williams and Yun-Joo Lee (2005), 'The minds of leaders: de-linking war and violence', this volume, p210.

[18] See Hinde (2005); M. S. Swaminathan (2003), 'Peace Dividend: Pathway to achieving UN Millennium Goals', and S. Brittan (2001), 'The Ethics and Economics of the arms trade', www.preparingforpeace.org. Samuel Brittan's paper was first delivered to the Royal Society of the Arts, Manufactures and Commerce in 2001 and was kindly donated to *Preparing for Peace* by the author.

[19] Swaminatham (2003).

[20] Swaminatham (2003).

[21] Hinde (2005) p. 93.

[22] Williams and Yun-Joo Lee (2005), p. 229.

[23] Swaminathan (2003).

[24] Rotblat (2001).

[25] Williams and Yun-Joo Lee (2005), p. 229

[26] See Cairns (2003) and P. Rogers (2005), 'The environmental costs of war', this volume, p. 157.

[27] Swaminathan (2003).

[28] Swaminathan (2003).

[29] Walker (2003).

[30] R. Goldstone, 'Prosecuting War Criminals', this volume, p. 197.

[31] Williams and Yun-Joo Lee(2005).

[32] P. Grossrieder (2005), 'The human costs of war', this volume, p. 150.

[33] Beach (2005), p. 106.

[34] Judge Richard Goldstone, p. 197.

[35] Judge Richard Goldstone, p. 207.

[36] Judge Richard Goldstone, p. 204.

[37] Grossrieder (2005), p. 142.

[38] R. S. McNamara, *In Retrospect* (Random House, 1995) p. 33.

[39] Walker (2003).

[40] Goldstone discusses changing attitudes towards casualties, attributing this to war crimes tribunals (2005, p. 207). Beach notes that in recent years 'the issue of proportionality has dominated at least the vocabulary of the debate', with everyone paying 'at least lip-service' to the consideration of non-combatant immunity (2005, p. 111).

[41] Current estimates for the numbers of Iraqi casualties vary from several thousand to tens of thousands. In October 2004, a controversial study published in the British Medical Journal *The Lancet* reported that the Iraqi population had suffered some 100,000 extra deaths since the invasion in 2003. In December 2004, forty-six eminent former military staff (including *Preparing for Peace* contributor General Sir Hugh Beach), former diplomats and members of the clergy wrote to Prime Minister Tony Blair requesting a formal enquiry into civilian casualties in Iraq.

[42] See Beach's analysis of the tactics and weapons used in Kosovo (2005, p. 114); and Walker's discussion of high-altitude bombing in Yugoslavia and Afghanistan (2003).

[43] Walker (2003). Walker goes on to conclude that, 'If two clauses fall, then all seven clauses fall in what its medieval authors designed as a seamless web.'

[44] Grossrieder (2005), p. 141.

[45] Grossrieder (2005), p. 146.

[46] Grossrieder (2005), p. 142. See also S. Castles (2001), 'Environmental Change and Forced Migration', www.preparingforpeace.org. Castles' paper was first delivered at Green College, Oxford, in 2001, and was kindly donated to *Preparing for Peace* by the author.

[47] Grossrieder (2005), p. 147.

[48] Rogers (2005), p. 158; Cairns (2003).

[49] Rogers (2005), p. 157.

[50] Cairns (2003).

[51] http://www.quaker.org.uk/peace/qpsdocs/nutsh2.html

[52] http://www.globalissues.org/Geopolitics/ArmsTrade/ BigBusiness.asp#Someadditionalnumbers

[53] http://news.bbc.co.uk/2/hi/business/3603923.stm

[54] Scientists for Global Responsibility (19 January 2005), *Soldiers in the Laboratory* http://www.sgr.org.uk/conferences.html

[55] Cairns (2003).

[56] Grossrieder (2005) p. 151.

[57] Elworthy (2001).

[58] Brittan (2001).

[59] Grossrieder (2005) p. 142.

[60] See Walker (2003), Cairns (2003), Swaminathan (2005), and C. Tickell (2005), 'The UN and the Future of Global Governance', this volume, pp. 189.

[61] Tickell (2005), p. 189.

[62] Cairns (2003).

Part Two: Alternative responses to the threat of war

[63] Tickell (2005), p. 181.

[64] Tickell (2005), p. 181.

[65] Cairns (2003).

[66] Cairns (2003).

[67] Wilkinson (2002).

[68] Wilkinson (2002).

[69] Sajid (2005), p. 126.

[70] Howard, 'War against Terrorism', (2001).

[71] Howard, 'War against Terrorism', (2001).

[72] Wilkinson (2002).

[73] Strachan (2002).

[74] M. van Creveld, 'War: Past, Present, Future', (2003). www.preparingfrpeace.org

[75] van Creveld.

[76] Rogers (2005).

[77] SWESI – Sutainable Water and Energy security Initiative in the MENA Region. http://www.trec-ecumena.org/swesci_web.htm

[78] Rogers (2005).

[79] Cairns (2003).

[80] Stewart, 'Development and Security', (2005), www.preparingforpeace.org.

[81] Stewart, 'Development and Security', (2005), www.preparingforpeace.org.

[82] Swaminathan (2003).

[83] Swaminathan (2003).

[84] Tickell (2005), p. 184.

[85] Castles, 'Environmental change and Forced Migration', (2001).

[86] Hinde (2005), p. 71.

[87] Solana, 'Effective multilateralism', (2004), www.preparingforpeace.org

[88] Grossrieder (2005), p. 151.

[89] Goldstone (2005), p. 207.

[90] Goldstone (2005), p. 201.

[91] Tickell (2005), p. 179.

[92] Walker (2005).

[93] Tickell (2005), p. 187.

[94] G. Monbiot, *The Age of Consent: a Manifesto for a New World Order* (Flamingo, 2003)

[95] UN Report of the High-level Panel on Threats, Challenges and Change, 2004

[96] Elworthy (2001).

[97] Elworthy (2001).

[98] Anstee, 'Leading a UN Mission: Angola 1992-93', www.preparingforpeace.org.

[99] Swaminathan (2003).

[100] Swaminathan (2003).

[101] J. Stiglitz, *Globalization and its discontents* (Penguin, 2002)

[102] Rotblat (2000).

[103] Hinde (2005), p. 85.

[104] Cairns (2003).

[105] Hinde (2005), p. 92.

[106] Sajid (2005) – (note, not in abridged version, this volume), www.preparingforpeace.org.

[107] Grossrieder (2005), p. 150.

[108] J. Schell, *The Unconquerable World: Power, Nonviolence and the Will of the People* (Allen Lane, 2004)

[109] Williams and Yun-Joo Lee(2005), p. 209.

[110] Williams and Yun-Joo Lee (2005), p. 244.

[111] Williams and Yun-Joo Lee (2005), p. 228.

Part Three: Conclusions

[112] Beach (2005), p. 116.